FOREWORD BY WILLIAM URY,
NEW YORK TIMES BESTSELLING AUTHOR OF *GETTING TO YES*

INTENTIONAL

AMBITION

REDEFINING YOUR WORK FOR GREATER JOY, FREEDOM, AND FULFILLMENT

RHA GODDESS

FOUNDER AND CEO OF MOVE THE CROWD

WILEY

Published by John Wiley & Sons, Inc., Hoboken, New Jersey.
Published simultaneously in Canada.

For general information on our other products and services or for technical support, please contact our Customer Care Department within the United States at (800) 762-2974, outside the United States at (317) 572-3993, or fax (317) 572-4002.

Wiley also publishes its books in a variety of electronic formats. Some content that appears in print may not be available in electronic formats. For more information about Wiley products, visit our web site at www.wiley.com.

Library of Congress Cataloging-in-Publication Data is available:

ISBN: 9781394299683 (cloth)
ISBN: 9781394299690 (ePub)
ISBN: 9781394299706 (ePDF)

Cover Design: Wiley
Cover Image: © Shpak Anton/Shutterstock
Author Photo: Courtesy of Sheldon Bolter Photography

SKY10100138_031425

For Zuri, Harlowe, Charles, Adana,
Matt, Benjamin, Ethan

And all my beloved future
generations … in honor of your ambition

Contents

Foreword   *vii*

Introduction: You See Resignation ... I See Renegotiation   *xi*

PART I   NEGOTIATION   **1**

1   You Say Career Wall, I Say Life Wall   **3**

2   Success as Sacrifice: An Unchallenged Story   **15**

**3   When Failure to Succeed Is Almost
       Guaranteed: Thwarting**   **27**

PART II   RESIGNATION   **41**

4   One Coin, Two Sides: Giving Up vs. Quitting   **43**

5   The Suck in Success   **57**

6   Wounded Ambitions and Wounding Ambition   **65**

PART III   RENEGOTIATION   **79**

7   Reclaiming: Whose Story Is It, Anyway?   **81**

8   Realigning: The Truth about Getting True   **91**

**9   Reimagining: A More Successful
       Definition of Success**   **105**

PART IV   HOW TO RENEGOTIATE WITH YOURSELF   117

10 Changing Your Mindset about Change   119

11 Signing Your Own Permission Slip   131

12 Cultivating Your True Ambition   143

PART V   HOW TO RENEGOTIATE WITH OTHERS   153

13 Setting Up Your Game Plan
        (and Guardrails) for Reentry   155

14 Coming to the Table Prepared   165

15 Overcoming the Scarcity Scare   177

PART VI   HOW TO RENEGOTIATE WITH THE WORLD   187

16 Renegotiating with the World:
        The "Yeah, But" Chapter   189

17 Who Wins? A Pep Talk to Send You on Your Way   199

        Notes   209

        Acknowledgments   213

        About the Author   217

        Index   221

Foreword

As an anthropologist and a mediator, I have enjoyed the opportunity to be a lifelong student and practitioner of negotiation—of all kinds: from family quarrels to labor strikes to peace negotiations around the world. So it is with distinct pleasure that I introduce a book by my dear friend Rha about what is perhaps the most important personal negotiation of our lives.

What does true success mean for each of us? How can we spend our working hours and not come to the end of our lives with a lump of regret that we did not have the courage to pursue what we truly want to do and offer this world? What is our calling? What is our gift? What will bring joy? Discovering the answers to these questions is what Rha calls "re-negotiation." It turns out to be key to our ultimate sense of fulfillment and satisfaction.

Rha's wise and practical message resonates deeply with me, leading me to reflect about my own life experience and the hard and valuable lessons I have learned along the way. I remember times when I felt I was on my path and other times when I felt I was straying away.

My first adult job was as a young assistant professor working at a business school. It had the allure of recognition, financial security, and a structured and comfortable path through life. But inside, I felt a certain hollowness. At the time, the Cold War between the United States and the Soviet Union was intensifying with the risk of an unthinkable nuclear conflagration. From childhood, it had been a troubling concern of mine—I could never understand why humans would be so foolish as to risk destroying everything we hold dear in life. I dreamed of finding a way to personally engage on this issue.

So, I left the business school—and all its promises—and took a chance creating a project on how to reduce the risk of an accidental nuclear war. Looking back four decades later through the prism of Rha's useful framework, I realize it was a "renegotiation" that served me and others well.

Reading *Intentional Ambition* calls to mind all the people I know who are on this journey of renegotiation as they grapple with the hard questions Rha raises. While the questions may be the same, the answer for each of us will be different. Rha has a way of speaking to each of us, in whatever phase of life we may find ourselves.

I reflect on my three children as each seeks to figure out the work that satisfies them and how to reconcile that with the life they want to lead. I think of colleagues like my friend Claire who this very week is faced with the unexpected challenge of leading a nonprofit and the travel it calls for while being available for her teenage daughter who is struggling at school. At the other end of life, I think of friends who are not wanting to retire yet but wish to renegotiate a new relationship with work.

I first had the pleasure of getting to know Rha in an unusual setting, walking through the contested land of Israel/Palestine in the footsteps of Abraham, the legendary ancestor of much of humanity. As we trod the ancient footpaths, we conversed deeply about life and the search for one's true calling. We remembered that Abraham's story too was of renegotiation. Well advanced in years, he heard an inner call that said: "Go. Go forth. Go find out who you really are." He mustered up the courage to leave the land of his forefathers in Mesopotamia and travel with his family in search of the Promised Land.

Renegotiating how we spend our lives turns out to be not just a timely modern question in these tumultuous times, but a question for the ages. On his journey, Abraham learned his true vocation which was to offer kind-hearted hospitality to strangers in need. And that is what he is known for to this day—embodied in the astonishing hospitality woven into the cultural fabric of the region, all conflict apart.

As Rha suggests in this valuable offering, there are three negotiations contained in this great renegotiation.

The first and perhaps the hardest negotiation is with ourselves. As we consider what we want in our lives, tension and conflict naturally arise within us—between, for example, our desire for security and our desire for fulfillment. How do we reconcile what seem to be opposing tugs? Here Rha offers us a framework for navigating these delicate internal negotiations—changing our mindset, confronting our fears, and granting ourselves permission to pursue a life of greater freedom, joy, and fulfillment. Renegotiation, it turns out, is an inside job, proceeding from the inside out.

The second negotiation is negotiating with others about the things that truly matter to us. How do we advance our dreams and implement our new terms and conditions in a way that enables us to meet our needs and at the same time address the concerns of others—whether it is our colleagues or our families and partners. How do we overcome what Rha calls the "Scarcity Scare"?

Foreword

The third and final negotiation has to do with the larger world. What contribution do we aspire to make to the community around us? How can our renegotiation serve as a model for others in helping transform the bigger systems that entrap so many of us? How can we help bring about the larger shifts in the world that we would like to see? Here Rha invites us to be heroic—in her own words, "to leverage our own growth and evolution for the good of the world."

What I love about Rha's book is its spirit of possibility and humble audacity. If not us, who, and if not now, when? You, my fellow reader, are in for a treat. I wish you every success in your own noble renegotiation.

—William Ury
New York Times best-selling author,
academic, anthropologist, negotiation
expert, and co-founder of the
Harvard Program on negotiation
November 2024

Introduction

You See Resignation ... I See Renegotiation

Have you ever been woken from a deep sleep and felt utterly disoriented? Jolted awake so violently, you didn't know where you were? It's unsettling, right? Especially if you didn't even realize you were sleeping.

I published my first book, *The Calling*—a guide to finding your purpose and getting paid to pursue it—in January 2020, when the world was a different place. We were pre-COVID. Pre-Ahmaud Arbery, pre-Breonna Taylor, pre-George Floyd. Pre-January 6 and the near end of American democracy. Back then, people got out of bed in the morning as they always had, commuted to work as they always did, and lived the lives they were accustomed to living. Business as usual.

Then everything changed, so much so, so joltingly, that instead of just getting out of bed, people started *waking up*—the kind of waking up where you can't make sense of where you are. And one of the things that made the least sense, because it was connected to every part of our lives, because it *ruled* our lives—was the way we work.

You know what I mean: that sacrificing way. Signing away our precious time and energy; forgoing our mental, spiritual, and physical well-being, squandering our true gifts; sanding down our natural contours—all in the name of chasing a vision of success that for so many is actually unattainable. Or that, if attained, so often feels like what's the point?

I think of the Great Resignation—that mass exodus of American workers, roughly 50 million in 2021 and then again in 2022—as our mutual primal scream upon waking up to a few radical truths: That life is short. That money isn't everything. That we want to show up and make a difference. That what we do isn't who we are, yet how we do it can be everything. And that business as usual isn't going to cut it anymore (and, if we're being honest, it never did). At a time of massive uncertainty about the future, the people who've resigned know two things for sure: We are not going back to the way we were, and we are not going back to the way we used to work.

Even if you haven't quit your job in the past few years, I suspect you've at least experienced the stirrings of such feelings. Maybe you've asked yourself: What am I doing this for? Why am I living like this? Is it worth it? Is it even what I want? And boy, do I get it. My own "no going back" moment took place 28 years ago, when I left corporate America to see if I could help others in search of a better way of living, working, and leading. Today, my coaching and consulting company, Move the Crowd, is one of the places people turn to when they feel as though they've hit the wall. We work with entrepreneurs and mid-level corporate managers, executive assistants and CEOs, budding social-media influencers, and leaders of nonprofit organizations—all kinds of people from all kinds of backgrounds, all of whom are seeking greater purpose and meaning. Recently, I've been paying special attention to one cohort in particular. Historically, they've been the most undervalued in the workplace and yet possibly, at this moment, have the most to offer: Women of color. My data shows that this group has been the most impacted by COVID (especially when we recognize the pressures on frontline workers and mothers, and the national racial reckoning). As such, they have a unique perspective on questioning the status quo and understanding how to make work more bearable—for everyone.

When journalists and analysts started writing about the Great Resignation, there was a lot of surprise involved: Millions of workers! Just up and quitting! Across all industries! Month after month! From where I sat, it was not nearly so surprising. In my view, this major cultural shift, though absolutely catalyzed by recent events, has been brewing for over two decades (just think about our world of work post-9/11). The entire time, I've been working with people who, in a culture that values work-based productivity above all else, have finally reached their breaking point.

Through Move The Crowd, I've helped tens of thousands of these people radically and thrillingly reset their lives by renegotiating their relationship to work: What they do, why they do it, and how to do it so it feels more meaningful and more aligned with who they really are. Demand for our services has grown dramatically as more and more people wake up to the certainty that they want—I would even say *need*—to do more with their work than just work. They want to contribute and be fulfilled. They want to be doing something *of value*, for which they want to *be valued*.

This is especially true for those who feel like being valued is a constant fight. Our most recent work with women of color (WOC) has only underscored this tipping point. They continue to be the most heavily impacted on all fronts post-pandemic (e.g. health, economic, social/political) and the most enthusiastic about the need for change. We've even developed seminars to help fed-up WOC executives architect their own emancipation plans. The results of the work have been game changing as the women who participate emerge with a whole new vision and blueprint for their life and their work. As word continues to spread about the impact, the demand for these seminars continues to grow. WOC are recognizing through this work that they can do it differently and on their own terms.

No one is happier than I am when one of my clients publishes a *New York Times* bestseller or gives a TED Talk that goes viral or wins a prestigious fellowship. But I see my greatest success as the countless people I've helped create a path to doing work that feels authentic and makes a meaningful contribution to the world—and doing it in a way that lets them go home happier at the end of the day, with more bandwidth to engage with their families. I've helped people give themselves permission to step off the corporate ladder (which for most people is more like a treadmill) to pursue their greatest passions and to prioritize their commitment to doing good both off the job and on.

I call this work—the work of transforming what it means to work—*renegotiating*.

I help people do it by helping them *radically rethink their beliefs about ambition and success*. They don't do this in a vacuum, but in the context of an evolving understanding of themselves, the world, their place in the world, and the entrenched and largely invisible systems that attempt to dictate who can succeed and on what terms. That, in a nutshell, is renegotiation, and the insights in this book will help you achieve it. Just as they helped me.

Where I'm Coming From

When my dad passed away in 2016, I was overwhelmed with grief, and my response was to double down on what I'd always done: Work. I threw myself into 20-hour days, stacked meetings back-to-back-to-back, and made my team members' business my business and their problems my own. Without realizing it, I grew a little more miserable every day, felt a little more trapped, and became a little more resentful.

That resentment started seeping into every interaction, no matter what or whom I was dealing with. Yet for the life of me, I couldn't understand how my dream of building my own company had become such a nightmare—until circumstances in the outer world (the white-supremacist riot in Charlottesville, Virginia; thorny racial and gender dynamics within my team; the entrepreneur's never-ending need to balance mission and revenue—to name just three) crashed into my pressure-cooker inner world, and *BAM*. It wasn't my first moment of awakening, but it was a big one. So big, it set me on a path to transforming—*renegotiating* the way I worked. That, in turn, transformed the way we work at Move The Crowd. And this renegotiation has now become central to the work we've helped so many people do—the very work this book is all about.

So, what *is* the work? In my case: I affirmed that I was in the right place—Move The Crowd was indeed my calling, my dream job—but I was going about it the wrong way. I had to take an honest look at how I'd been working—and hence living. I had to untangle my identity from a way of working that didn't align with or fulfill me. I had to get real with who I was and what I could and could not tolerate. I had to get radically honest about my ambition. Why was I *really* doing what I was doing? What did I really want? Was success really what I'd thought it was? Was the kind of success I'd bought into even possible? I had to connect the dots between my inner and outer worlds, and when I did, I came to understand that the way I'd overworked myself as a way of hiding from grief wasn't so different from the way I'd always worked—it was only a matter of degree.

And further, my lifelong work MO was tangled up in the unconscious urgency I felt to redeem my father's legacy as a Black man who'd grown up during Jim Crow, intertwined with his deeply ingrained assumptions about survival and success. I came to discover that I was terrified that I would never be able to work hard enough to create the change I wanted or to receive my proper due.

Informed by this new understanding of myself in relation to the world, I then had to give myself permission to forge a new and better way of working—of *being*. That new way involved honoring my gut-wisdom about people and situations; accepting (*really* accepting) less than constant perfection; and setting boundaries—mental, spiritual, emotional, financial—that allowed me to put my own well-being first. It was about telling myself the truth about who and what was for me, and who and what was not.

In all of this, I was bolstered by a new sense of clarity about how our system of work perpetuates itself. How it tries to convince us— falsely—that we are what we do. How it deceives us into thinking we have no choice but to do its bidding.

None of this, of course, happened overnight. It was definitely a process. But it was a process I emerged from with an electric sense of renewal. Instead of wanting to pull the covers over my head in the morning, I was eager to get going. At work, I was tuned in, present, focused, and it was an expansive kind of focus. I felt as though I was going through my days in 360 degrees, receptive to new ideas that might come from anywhere, connecting dots in new and fruitful ways. I had silence and room to breathe. I was more creative at troubleshooting and solving problems. Above all, I was *happier!*

But enough about me. We're here to get *you* happier, more engaged, and more fully alive, where *you* wake up feeling not just ready but actually inspired for each new day.

Renegotiation, Step-by-Step

This book will guide you through the same steps that I and so many Move The Crowd clients have undertaken to renegotiate their relationship to work, and therefore to life—a renegotiation based on redefining, on a personal level, what I call true ambition and success.

As you work through these steps, you can download more tools and resources at www.movethecrowd.me/IA-resources.

The initial steps focus on getting your bearings.

Negotiation is the give-and-take process we think we're signing up for when we're striving for conventional success. We work hard, we pay our dues, we climb the ladder, we get the prize, and we live happily and wealthily ever after. But there's a reason it's called a "success story." For almost all of us, this version of success *is* just a story, a myth. In our secular culture, it's almost a religion, and success stories are its parables. Unfortunately, these stories tend to have two gaping holes. First, they gloss over the sacrifices, often very deep and very painful, that so many of us are asked to make in pursuit of success— the wheeling and dealing we do *with ourselves* as we try to negotiate or navigate our way upward. Second, they fail to acknowledge that for vast numbers of us, the deck is stacked against us in such a way that our failure to succeed is almost guaranteed from the start. I call this *thwarting*, a term you'll come to know well.

The work you'll do in thinking about Negotiation is twofold. One, you'll identify the things you've forfeited as you people-pleased and team-played your way toward your dream job. Two, you'll consider thwarting and the baked-in systems designed to limit access to success. I'll help you discern where you fit into those systems and reckon with whether you want to continue being part of them—all the while acknowledging that conventional success stories originated in a different time, a time when the road to opportunity was not open to all but rather blocked by a narrow and jealously guarded gate.

Realizing that what you were striving for hasn't happened—and, for reasons that are now more readily apparent, may never happen—brings us to stage two on our continuum: *Resignation*. But which kind? In the old paradigm, resignation meant *being* resigned. *Grin and bear it. It's a living. It is what it is.* Then there's what I call Resignation 2.0: the Great Resignation kind of resignation, where you've had enough and you need out, *now*, even if no new job is waiting for you. The difference between the two types of resignation is partly a matter of the times we're living through and partly—hugely—a matter of you. Here we'll get acquainted with the concept of the tolerance threshold: the point at which the distance between where you are and who you are becomes untenable. And you'll have a chance to explore your own, because every person's tolerance threshold is unique.

We'll also dig into the destructive belief—fostered by our system of work—that your job is your identity. Not true! Far too many miserable workers have stayed put in their misery because they don't know who they'd *be* if they weren't doing what they *do*. This is especially true for people who are, according to conventional wisdom, successful. The more money you make, the higher you climb on whatever ladder you're climbing, the more you tend to believe that your job is you, as opposed to being just one of innumerable things *about* you. (And in all probability not the most important one.) This is one of a few reasons why success can sometimes suck. We'll get into those reasons in a productive way.

Untangling your identity and your job paves the way for a more complicated untangling: of you and your ambitions. So often our seeming aspirations are actually other people's expectations—a parent, a spouse, the culture at large; it could be anyone. Or, as in my case, and often with no conscious awareness, we do what we do, the way we do it, because we're trying to right a past wrong or fulfill a legacy or do someone else's do-over. That might sound noble, but it's no way to live. My best definition of a worthy ambition? Following your own ambition. I'll guide you through an ambition inventory that will give you an accurate understanding of what can and does truly motivate you.

What comes next is where *Renegotiation* begins—the work I do best, the work I'm going to share with you. And it starts with *reclaiming* the stories we tell ourselves about ourselves. These stories have a profound impact on how we move through life, and they reflect everything we experience in life—the good, the bad, the memorable, the regrettable. Something happens, we process it a certain way, and we draw conclusions about what it says about us. These conclusions become our stories, our narratives. When they're inspiring and serve a positive role, that's great. But when they're rooted in dysfunction, it's trouble.

Reclaiming your personal story is one part of preparing to craft a new success story. The other part is stepping back to do what I call an alignment check, to confirm the core values you'll want to be syncing up with. With those values top of mind, you can then begin to reimagine what real success, meaningful success, will look like for you. You'll get granular about the ideal *who*, *what*, *when*, *where*, and *how* of your work and your life, in a way that is inspiring to *you*.

Of course, we're not just here to tell stories. The goal is to turn your success story into reality—which brings us to the real nitty gritty of this book: the how-to. It's one thing to *understand* renegotiation, but how do you actually *do* it?

My answers come in two parts: one involving renegotiating with other people and institutions, and the other—which in some ways is trickier!—involving renegotiating with yourself.

Since I love a challenge, we'll start with the trickiest part of the tricky one. It is perhaps the most important part of renegotiation: changing your mindset about the possibility of change. In the Resignation phase, when it seems as though your two options are either stick it out and be miserable, or quit, it's easy to forget that—just like success stories—our whole system of work is a creation, based on manmade structures, and that what was made can be unmade and indeed remade. I'll help you challenge your beliefs about change (often inherited) and examine your attitude toward risk (also often inherited). And we'll take a page from the millennial/Gen Z playbook—the "Says who?" generation—as you work to accept your own agency and power.

"Says who?" also applies to our next step, which is all about permission—specifically, giving yourself permission to matter.

I will show you that giving yourself permission to matter is about giving yourself five individual permissions: to want what you really want, to pursue your goal, to be a work in progress (what I call being on the journey), to succeed or fail on your terms, and to be supported in the ways you truly need to be.

Next, we'll turn to the how-to of renegotiating with others. I'll give you tools and a game plan for reentry. This includes setting boundaries—oh, how I love a good boundary! I think of them as guardrails on the road to happiness and true success. I'll also give you a fantastic tool for doing the thing that scares so many of my clients: actual negotiating.

Part of what makes real negotiating intimidating is that our economy—really, our entire culture—is based on the notion of scarcity. You ask for something and are told there's not enough. Not enough room at the table, let alone at the top. Not enough profit to share. It's used to foster competition rather than collaboration and cooperation. A win for you is a loss for me.

We'll examine the scarcity scare, considering all the ways that it's a myth. The scarcity mindset wants us to believe that there simply aren't resources to fairly compensate, promote, value, and appreciate women of color—that more for them would mean less for others. In fact, our data demonstrates the opposite: that women of color are a massively underutilized resource at a time when their wisdom, skills, and insights are sorely needed and could benefit entire divisions, entire companies, and an entire economy. That's the truth I want to share: that making work better for some of us makes things better for all of us.

The Bottom Line

Over the course of a lifetime, the average American will spend some 90,000 hours at work. *90,000 hours.* If you love what you do and how you're doing it, those hours will be a blessing. If not, they'll be a slow and steady selling of your soul. A bit of your soul every day, in exchange for a job that doesn't make you happy.

For so many years, millions of Americans viewed that exchange as necessary, inevitable, unavoidable. We were, in a word, resigned.

Then, in the past few years, many of us went from being resigned to resigning. Now, whether or not you've walked away from a job, it's time for the next step: re-signing. As in making a new contract with yourself for who you'll be and how you'll work, drawing up new terms for what you are and are not willing to do, for how work will fit into the rest of your life, for how it will align with your true ambitions and reflect a more vibrant relationship to the world. In a word, *renegotiating*.

All of this is the work of *Intentional Ambition*. And it just might be the most important work you'll ever do. Because if you're living for the end of the work day, for the arrival of the weekend, for the can't-come-a-minute-too-soon vacation that will finally be here next month, then what you're really doing is wishing this day away, wishing this week away, wishing this month away. In other words, *wishing your life away*. You're on the "wake me when it's over" plan—with your *life*. I don't want to live that way, and I know you don't either.

This book is a guide to avoiding those regrets—to seeing through and beyond the systemic structures and ingrained beliefs that make work so unrewarding for so many. It's a book for people who've woken up to the hard truth that buying into business as usual comes at a price, and that price is just too steep. It's a book for people who know they can't go back but aren't quite sure how to go forward. It's a book for people who believe that, as Brené Brown has said, "You cannot change the world if you don't change the way we work." It's the book I wish I'd had when I was stumbling through my own renegotiation. I wrote it to help you move—with grace, with purpose, with optimism, and even with joy—through yours. So what are we waiting for?

Part I

Negotiation

Chapter 1

You Say Career Wall, I Say Life Wall

"I feel like I've been so deep in this grind of how the heck do I make this work that I've lost sight of why I'm even doing it."
—AG, Corporate & Entrepreneurial Event Producer

G rowing up, I always wanted to be a doctor. I'd play the game Operation for hours, trying to remove the problematic parts from that poor man's body without setting off the buzzer and making his nose light up. Let's just say it's a good thing I didn't become a surgeon.

The funny thing is, playing that game foreshadowed the work I do today: helping people live happier, more fulfilling lives by helping them identify and remove the problematic parts. It turns out that this work actually does have something in common with doctoring, in the sense that it starts with the right diagnosis.

When people come to me, they're usually struggling, but they often don't know what they're struggling *with*. So, I take their history, ask *lots* of questions, and deeply observe their behaviors to make an accurate assessment and prescribe the right course of treatment. I take this part of my work very seriously because I can't help cure what ails them if I don't get the diagnosis right.

Most of my clients come to me believing that their problem is with work. They've hit a career wall. They think their job or business is—or was—the cause of their burnout, chronic anxiety, insomnia, or panic attacks. They believe their inability to achieve the goals they set for themselves is the result of some failure or lack on their part. They think they've hit a career wall and they have the bumps and bruises (in the form of stress, migraines, high-blood pressure, you name it) to prove it. But even though those bumps and bruises are real, the work—either what they're doing or how they're doing it—is only *a* problem. It's not *the* problem. Just like the physical, emotional, psychological, and spiritual dilemmas it leads to, unhappiness with work is itself a symptom of something deeper. And like any symptom, it will persist until the underlying challenge is identified and resolved.

So, what then, is the underlying issue? I've found that many of us have a *dysfunctional relationship with ambition*, which comes from a distorted perception of who we really are and a debilitating definition of success. The goals that dictate the course of our existence are literally making us sick. The wall we're hitting is not a career wall. It's a life wall.

The Problem with Our Ambition

In our country, the culture of work is built on a skewed relationship with ambition, or, as I think of it, *wanting*. There's often a disconnect between what we say we want versus what we really want (the doctor who longed to be a painter but didn't want to disappoint her parents). There's often a gap between what's seen as "acceptable" to want versus what is not (the manager who'd be so much happier being managed); this gap is usually occupied by fear or shame. There are things we don't allow ourselves to even admit we want because, usually without realizing it, we don't believe we'll ever achieve it or many times we question if we're even worthy. We try to fill what's wanting (missing) from our lives by wanting (desiring) things that won't actually fill the void. Often, we wind up wanting what's perceived as acceptable, and we push our own desires aside. Furthermore, we adopt the dictated habits and actions that support these "respectable" desires (being the first one in the office and the last one to leave, for example).

All of this causes us to lose touch with ourselves. And because we've lost touch with who we really are and what we really need, we don't understand what motivates us to pursue what we *really* want. We avoid thinking about how much we're willing to compromise to get it. And we don't stop to consciously consider how we'll know—and feel—when we've achieved it.

When I first started hearing stories about the "Great Resignation" in 2020, I was fascinated but not surprised. Millions of people were quitting their jobs en masse, month over month, across all industries. Journalists and analysts and experts seemed to find the phenomenon shocking and reported on it incredulously—how could so many people quit their jobs with no other prospects? In the middle of a pandemic, no less?

The media painted workers as simply being "burnt out" and—in the wake of the reassessing that the pandemic provoked—deciding that they wanted more: more pay, more flexibility, more overall happiness. While on the surface this may be true, there are layers upon layers of lived experience that have brought so many to the brink.

Beyond all the data and estimations are the harsh realities of what people have endured over the last 25 years in a culture that has demanded work-based productivity above all else—joy, health, family, you name

5

it. The growing demands on the average worker in the face of diminishing wages, toxic corporate cultures, and stalled professional mobility have finally reached a breaking point. And even as we examine the current state, post-pandemic, we apparently have graduated from the Great Resignation to the Great Gloom! According to Bamboo HR's June 2023 findings, employee dissatisfaction was at an all-time high with evaluations plummeting "with no indication of slowing down."

> Bamboo's findings were drawn from more than 1,600 companies tracking more than 1.4 billion employee Net Promoter Score (eNPS) entries. The BambooHR report also quoted a recent Gallup study where they found that 80 percent of employees were dissatisfied with their current jobs.

So, what have we been through over the last 25 years that might warrant this massive upheaval? Over the last two decades we've had three major blows to our economy (i.e. work stability and security) all rooted in some form of tragedy. From 9/11 in 2001 to the Great Recession in the late 2000s to the COVID-19 pandemic in 2020, the last 25 years have given us so much volatility and uncertainty that the average worker has been pivoting like a ballerina on steroids just to keep their head above water. And this is not just low-wage workers; when we dig into the realities of high-level executives we see the trade of better wages in exchange for way more stress and far less life. If we layer on all of the global and regional conflicts, the rise in identity-based violence, massive corruption on the part of political and business leaders, and not-so-random mass shootings, there is something way more troubling brewing underneath the surface of our daily realities. To quote the wisdom of nFormation's PowHer Redefined report, We aren't just burnt out, we're traumatized! Many of us are mentally, physically, and emotionally stretched far beyond what is feasible, and quite frankly, people have had it!

But even while we experience this precarious, overstretched, and overstressed reality, we're still being driven, constantly pushed, and encouraged to strive for *more*. This quest for more has caused us to question: *What are we really doing all of this striving for?*

I remember the first time I met Megan. She was a high-level executive *and* a new mother who spent the bulk of her maternity leave trying to help her division hold it together. She came into the Zoom room in the heat of the pandemic looking sharp but barely able to hold her head up. "I'm exhausted," she said—then looked off into the distance as if the horizon might offer some relief. We sat in silence like that for a bit. "I know that what I'm doing is not what I'm meant to be," she finally said. "But I don't know how to get out." Megan's breaking point involved her year-end bonus; she was about to start negotiating it, and the clues being dropped by management were telling her not to get her hopes up. "It isn't about the money really," she told me. "It's just that money is the only language they understand. It's about them recognizing everything I gave up this year to deliver and the genuine acknowledgment of the value of my efforts. I talked to my boss and I can already tell it's going be a fight. So, if I've got to get ready to do battle, then I don't just want my bonus—I want out."

For Gavone, the breaking point was his health. After 22 years in the management-consulting world, living on trains, planes, and automobiles, never having a life or identity outside of the firm, he woke up one morning in Seattle, where he was working on a client project, and found that he literally couldn't get up. He'd been nursing a sense of low-grade exhaustion for years; any visit to the doctor came up with prescriptions for slightly stronger antacids, a firm slap on the shoulder, and an admonition to "get some rest." But the kind of rest he needed was way beyond his own comprehension. Making matters worse, he'd just inherited a new boss, and word on the street was that "she was not a fan" of him or his team. The level of anxiety he was carrying manifested itself in his rapid-fire speech and inability to stand still. He'd been battling insomnia for nearly six weeks. "I know I'm on my way to being a prime candidate for a heart attack—I can just feel it," he told me. "And the worst part is I'm not even clear about what I'm chasing anymore."

For Antoné, it was having to go into the field during the height of the contagion. "In the beginning, they told me that I wouldn't have to do it, but the more vocal I became about other issues, the more they started harping on the need for me to go out there." He smirked, "When I asked them if there was any way I could monitor the stations remotely, they assured me there wasn't. But I found a way to do it without their help, which just left me feeling like they didn't really care about my well-being. As a matter of fact I think this was their way of trying to get me to quit."

The Great Resignation has been a response to our skewed relationship to work and the long-standing expectation that for most of us, work has traditionally been this all-consuming barrage of demands we try our best to survive and get through: the ingrained knee-jerk reaction to bury our own wants, needs, desires, and voices, as the work keeps piling up; the almost unanimous agreement to live each day in fear of how we will be perceived and ultimately valued as we try to determine if we're on the "ins" or the "outs"; the relentless pressure to navigate the ever-shifting terrain of somebody else's playing field while trying to succeed and advance according to those ever-elusive rules has finally caught up. All that *wanting* has turned into an overwhelming, undeniable *I want out*.

Our relationship with work has been shaped by all of the messages we've received and by the examples we've witnessed over time. It's influenced by our perceived station in life and by the degree to which we believe that station is malleable. It's also shaped by our perception of the state of our external world and the way the impending doom on the five o'clock news finds its way to our front door. So when I say, life wall, I really mean it. This never-ending cycle of striving to meet this (debilitating, elusive, hollow, you name it) standard of success which is meant to define our status, viability, and credibility (aka worthiness) impacts every facet of the quality of our existence. And if we don't get underneath what's driving all of this, we may never get to a place in life or work where we truly feel happy or fulfilled.

The Negotiation-Resignation-Renegotiation Continuum

In order to chart the path for where we want to go, it's important to understand where we've been, who we've been and why it's led so many of us to the brink.

You Say Negotiation, I Say Navigation

When we set off at the genesis of our professional career, we enter into what I call the **Negotiation phase**. This is the phase where we arrive on the frontlines with great enthusiasm ready to embark on the grand adventure of our profession. Our primary aims in this phase are to learn the ropes by identifying what the standard of success is and determining what's required of us to meet that standard.

When we are Negotiating, we've already accepted that the game is mostly going to be played on somebody else's terms, i.e. on the terms of those who set (the table) and define the standard. Our intention is to try to get as close as we can to that standard while at the same time minimizing our level of risk. We tell ourselves it's necessary to make concessions in order to reap the rewards—and that's how the Negotiation (as in Navigation) begins. As we play the game of concession/reward, we are deep in the trade, operating with the belief that somehow, some way, we'll end up on top. We'll feel as though we have achieved something important. We'll be the hero, and others will look to us as successful—as if we've finally arrived. We'll be acknowledged, we'll be respected, and we'll be worthy to be praised.

But over time, as the terrain shifts, as priorities change on all sides, and as the demands for greater, more dramatic concessions arise, we start to question whether the standard is all it's cracked up to be. When we reach this point of reckoning in the Negotiation phase, we start to realize that most of our wheeling and dealing has been with *ourselves;* trading in ways that have left us feeling angry, frustrated, and even bankrupt (philosophically, morally, energetically, you name it). No matter how we arrive at that point, there is a moment when we each look ourselves in the eye and consciously choose—either to keep going along to get along or move in a totally different (i.e. new and sometimes terrifying) direction.

Are You Resigned or Did You Resign?

If we choose to consciously Negotiate (aka Navigate) as in go along to get along, that puts us into the **Resignation phase**. When we are Resigned, it means we have accepted that the standard of success for us in this situation is unachievable or is no longer desired. Initially, the Resignation is internal and represents our succumbing to the apathy we feel about the situation and more often about the people involved. They will not see us. They will not honor us. They will not invest in us. They will not advance us. The situation is hopeless and will not change. We will not get the opportunity to be heroic here. In the traditional definition of resignation, we give up—on the people, the situation, and sometimes even ourselves. But we stay in the same place, literally and metaphorically, nurturing our disappointment. This form of resignation can last for two minutes (as a precursor to Resignation 2.0) or for decades. We can spend endless years just going through the motions hoping and praying that things will get better.

But for some, at some point, in our many stages of grief, we get pissed! And, as we turn inward to face the alienation and isolation we feel, we awaken, and we begin to recognize the cost of our previous negotiations (aka navigations) and the things we traded that ultimately may not have been good for us. We start to examine the things we've sacrificed and endured and we move into a different form of Resignation, the one that has us say, "That's it!" And we do whatever we have to do to make a change. We finally let go—we quit or get fired or even just put our foot down right where we are. Some of us do it quietly, and some of us do it loud and proud. In this stage, *quitting is actually part of waking up.*

Why Renegotiation Is Essential

Quitting can be tricky. When we do, in the moment we may feel high, giddy even, but when the adrenaline rush subsides, it can leave us feeling lost and thinking "Now what?" That brings us to the **Renegotiation phase.**

This phase begins with some courageous soul searching and calls for new definitions for work and success. When we are renegotiating, we're coming to the table with a whole new set of terms. We're looking to be met eye to eye and, dare I say, heart to heart. We embrace the fact that we are older, wiser, and that our lived experience gives us a more wide-eyed approach to new opportunities. We bring our optimism, but we are also grounded in where the guardrails are when it comes to our values and willingness to sign on. When we renegotiate, we are seeking alignment and affirmation that who we are and what we stand for is welcome here. We bring our desire to be inspired, and we bring our desire to be heroic—with a deepened more seasoned understanding of what is required for us to contribute and shine.

Now that you understand each phase (negotiation, resignation, and renegotiation), you can start to observe where you are in your process. Notice what's informing your decisions in real time. You may find that as you take an inventory, you are at different stages in different areas of your life and work. For example, you may be in the Negotiation phase in your work but in the Resignation phase in an intimate love relationship. You may be in the Resignation phase when it comes to an old circle of friends, but in the Renegotiation phase when it comes to your health and well-being.

The gift of hitting your career wall is that it's bound to illuminate what is or isn't happening in every other area of your life. The invitation to Renegotiation doesn't just impact your work and the way you work; it affects the way you define and pursue any form of ambition and desired success. No matter where you are in the journey, you cannot get to Renegotiation without moving through Resignation, and you can't arrive at Resignation without first experiencing the effects of Negotiation (aka Navigation). The more you can understand about how you arrived at your current state and the motivations that got you there, the more you can leverage that awareness to help shape and inform how you'd like to move forward. So I want you to consider right now, where have you sacrificed in order to succeed?

Your Terms

Journal Exercise:

1. Where are you? Take a moment to identify where along the continuum you may be as you think about your own life and work.

2. As you respond to question 1, notice how you *feel* about the stage in the continuum you've chosen and choices you've made thus far.

3. As you consider where you are right now in your own life and work, is there an opportunity for Renegotiation? If so, where? Try to be as specific here as you can.

For more downloadable tools and resources, go to: www.move thecrowd.me/IA-resources.

Chapter 2

Success as Sacrifice: An Unchallenged Story

"When you're building a company, you're in the hustle—you make tons of sacrifices. For me—the biggest was not being present for my wife during a difficult labor with our first child. I actually gave a business presentation from her hospital room—I still regret this one."

—Anonymous

Nobody grows up wanting to be *un*successful. No matter where you come from, you're taught at a very young age to strive for a high ideal. You want to be a *big* success! A *huge* success! Rags to riches or already rich to even richer—anyone and everyone can make it big here in the land of opportunity.

Success is a story we're raised on, and we all buy into without realizing what we're buying. That's how we set out when we begin our working lives: full of hope and promise. We believe we're on the path to being the hero of the story and that our fate is in our hands—if not now then at least someday.

But almost from the beginning, the reality is different. Many of us do *not* become the hero of our own stories. Our efforts aren't met with the rewards we dreamed of, ever. In the give-and-take of work culture, you give, and they take. From where you part your hair to how much of your natural accent you retain to how much of your child's childhood you'll have time to experience, our system of work never stops asking for concessions.

Want to know what it feels like to Negotiate (as in Navigate)? Consider these real-life examples of the kinds of sacrifices we're asked to make in order to succeed:

- "I was told: 'You need to fix your face. People can see what you're thinking.'"

- "I was told: 'He thinks you don't like him—that you're out to get him. You need to set his mind at ease.'"

- "I was told that this is a free country: 'He can say whatever he wants. You just have to learn how to get along with him.'"

- "She suggested that maybe I should wear a black or gray hijab instead of 'all those vibrant colors,' so people would take me seriously."

- "They suggested that I speak less. Be more concise. Take up less space."

- "Not only did they overlook me for the promotion and give it to someone else—they asked me to train him to make sure he succeeded."

- "When she's unhappy, she shouts, and when she shouts, I just have to stand there and take it."

- "With the loss of my colleague, I now had to be on the phone with international at 2 a.m., then up at 5 a.m. to care for the kids, then work until 11 p.m. Without even so much as an acknowledgment that this was going above and beyond."

- "My leaders turned to me [a Black woman] in the executive meeting and asked, 'What should we do about the whole George Floyd thing? Can you put together a plan?'"
- "My father was dying, and all they cared about was whether they were going to get those revisions on time."
- "They packed the itinerary back-to-back with no time to grab food or even go to the bathroom. When I asked about the possibility of taking a break, they responded 'Yeah, good idea, and while you're out can you pick up food for the group?'"
- "When I walked through my duties with my supervisor and demonstrated that I should have been at both a higher title and pay scale, she looked at me and said, 'You're right,' and that was the last I heard about a raise."
- "This guy has been a disaster since the moment he got here, but because he is a friend of the CTO, we all have to put up with his outrageous behavior."

Violations like these are obviously painful and disorienting in the moment—an acute kind of pain that can wreck your day or your week. It's even worse when they keep coming; there's a cumulative effect that, over time, can alienate us from our sense of ourselves—who we are, what we believe, what we deserve. We start to become two people: the real us, outside of work, and the work us, who sucks it up because we need that job or we want that promotion or we believe it won't be like this forever. There is an erosion of agency and individuality and identity, until we're essentially wearing a uniform even if we're not.

Even when these violations get called out, the best-case-scenario response is usually a few more coins, or some other ill-conceived concession which is magically supposed to solve everything—but it doesn't. The more of ourselves we give away, the more we're asked to give. The more we're asked to give, the more we begin to detach from our humanity. The more we detach from our humanity, the easier it becomes to mistreat ourselves, mistreat others, or stand by in the face of others' mistreatment.

Let's look at a real-world example: Portia was considered a total rock star in her division. When she started with her company she came out of the gate really strong, receiving all kinds of awards and accolades for her performance. Then the company changed leadership and began restructuring and Portia got to see her boss less and less. "All of a sudden, I went from being the center of attention to basically, being left out of the loop." She sighed, "There were all these changes happening and I could barely keep up. When I approached my manager, she'd tell me not to worry about it. Then one day, I get a text from a colleague who tells me that they heard in a meeting that my company would be bringing in a new head of product development and that he would be starting on Monday. 'Did they give you a new role?' she asked me. How do I answer that question and not look ridiculous? What I found out was they replaced me overnight in the role and never even bothered to tell me. Then they had the nerve to tell me how much I was valued and asked me if there was something else I might want to do. So now, I've got to face my team, tell them I've been ousted, and help the company figure out what to do with me."

As much as we admire the external trappings of success from afar, it's important to recognize that we rarely know the whole story and may

Intentional Ambition

never fully understand the nature of the sacrifice nor the degree to which those perceptions of success actually represent reality.

What makes these experiences of painful sacrifice so pervasive? I can sum it up in two words—low expectations. When we step into professional environments, no matter what our roles are, we often expect to work like a dog, we expect there to be personality politics, we expect our clients to be unreasonable and our supervisors or managers to be overwhelmed, or we expect the company not to care about anything other than the bottom line. And we act in accordance with those expectations. If anything to the contrary shows up, we are pleasantly, daringly, shocked and surprised. When it comes to the culture of our workplace environments, our terms for participating, and that blessed trade, we have actually set the lowest standards for Negotiation possible.

Even more disappointing is the realization that the higher you go, the worse it gets. It's like that feeling of triumph you get having climbed to the top of a mountain only to realize how thin the air is? How poor the visibility is (pun intended)? How horrible and unsafe the conditions are? That you've made it to the peak only to discover that the sacrificing doesn't stop—but actually becomes more severe? And this challenge doesn't just exist in the corporate world; it can be found everywhere.

> For example, for Elise, who took the helm of a well-heeled arts organization, she quickly found that cause-related institutions were not immune. "I mean, I was at odds with the board from day one," she said. "The organization was struggling, and no one on the board was really doing anything to turn it around. From the initial meeting after I was hired, the games began. When I presented the

19

strategic plan, they fought it. They challenged every goal, questioned every personnel change, and did everything short of telling me there was no way that I could achieve what I aimed to achieve. I mean, we were already operating at a deficit, and somehow, they magically expected me to close the gap overnight—without making any substantive changes. When I asked them what they intended to contribute and/or raise in connection with our annual gala, they looked at me like I had two heads. I hadn't even had the role for more than 5 minutes and I could already tell I was going to have my work cut out for me just with the board alone, not to mention all of the other organizational challenges."

Some of us are able to transform these challenges into personal and professional growth while others are carrying past hurts and disappointments that remain unresolved even as we climb. What's worse, if we've resigned—as in quit—without having done that postmortem work, we may be enthusiastically dragging these experiences and our low expectations from one place to another, which can make us the victim in one scenario and the perpetrator in another.

Hard Work as the Holy Grail

So why are our stories of success or the pursuit thereof so riddled with pain? I know what I'm about to say will be taken by some as an absolute no-no, but I'm going here anyway. That's right, I am interrogating our relationship to working *hard*. This globalized agreement to grind-until-you-drop permeates every sector of our society and causes so many of us to sacrifice joy, vital organs, and even sacred connection for the perception of being "successful." But *why*?

This ethic of hard work runs deep. It's embedded in many religious, cultural, and free market ideals—so much so that there is little to no escape. The expectation of fierce effort in pursuit of any aspiration is the norm. Not only is it normalized, but it's *idolized*. And because it's idolized, there is enormous pressure to follow suit. When you layer in identity, lineage, and tradition, it becomes even more challenging to loosen the grip.

When I hit my life wall in 2017, I had to take a very serious look at *how* I was working. It took me years to unpack all of the conscious and not so conscious things I was being driven by. At the time my business had been growing, and in order to keep up with the demand, I had quite naturally begun working harder. I also expanded my team to help carry the load. The expanded team meant even more demands on my time because now I'm not just doing the work, I'm guiding, overseeing, and managing others. And because I was totally bought into the culture of "the grind" and "the hustle," I kept telling myself, "You've got this." Rising early, working late, eating … maybe. I had very little room to evaluate what was happening because my calendar was stacked with back to backs. Add into the mix my unprocessed grief over the loss of my father just four months before and some very messy family dynamics around the estate and you have a recipe for—you guessed it, disaster.

When I look back on this moment, I can clearly see how the narrative of hard work became central to what informed my choices. Success meant working really hard and giving up any form of perceived "comfort" to achieve the goal. It was all about doing whatever it took to get the result. Through it all, I kept telling myself, "You're not working hard enough, because you didn't get x, y, z, done" or "Let's just get this done before you break for dinner," but then four hours later, I was still at it. The scary part is there was nothing about this

Success as Sacrifice: An Unchallenged Story

that seemed wrong to me. This was just the way it was, and it was my job to extract the "gold" in exchange for my labor. The problem was, I had no idea then (and even now) just what the "gold" was that I was trying to extract. I, like so many of us, was simply trying to survive all of the expectations and demands that were being placed on me day after day.

When Sacrifice Becomes a Badge of Honor

The messages we receive about work begin at such a young age. Whether we witness the unrelenting labor of an elder or we ourselves are put to work when we were kids, we form our expectations and assumptions about what it's supposed to be very early. More often than not, those messages and examples firmly establish themselves as our norm.

When we consider the legacies many of us come from, whatever we endure is perceived to be a picnic compared to the challenges of those who have come before us. How do you compete with slavery? Indentured servitude? Labor camps? Or political asylum? These legacies are rooted in the pride associated with enduring unspeakable harm and abuse. Do we really want this to be the baseline for how we evaluate our own merit? Should this be the reason why we push ourselves so hard or the rationale for why we put up with inhumane expectations and treatment? There is a fine line between "sacrifice" and "suffering," and we blur that line more often than many of us would care to admit. Moreover, when we draw validation and credibility from tolerating the indignities, we set a precedent that perpetuates this cycle of work abuse.

When I could not go forward in 2017, I drew on these legacies of endurance and martyrdom until there became a point when I literally could not get up. And the work to repair the stress of all that grinding, toiling, and suffering taught me to hold these legacies with far less pride and far more compassion.

Do not get me wrong. There is nothing wrong with purposeful and inspired effort toward a dream or aspiration. But the deeply ingrained distortion of this extreme endurance and suffering narrative in the name of success as a badge of honor has become the source of much of the profound mental, spiritual, and emotional burnout and breakdown we find plaguing this epidemic of Resignation in our post-pandemic world. And we now have the science to prove it; we are not effective when we are utterly exhausted.

The 40-hour work week was legalized in 1940 after a century of tension between workers and employers to reduce the number of work hours (from 80 to 100 hours per week in the early 1800s). Just as with Henry Ford's research that popularized the 40-hour work week in 1926, data published by the Organization for Economic Cooperation and Development (OECD) in 2015 established that countries with longer work weeks (i.e. those close to 40 hours) were actually less productive according to their corresponding GDP per hour worked. In the study, Luxembourg led with a 29-hour work week.[1,2]

This "hard work" ethos has saturated our global culture and tells us that it is the price we must pay in order to succeed. We must sacrifice, we must endure, we must work hard, and the harder we work, the more worthy we potentially become of whatever it is we are pursuing.

When I truly decided to transform my way of working, I had to take my work ethic back to the studs. I had to ask myself what it was that

I wanted to be driven by, who it was that I wanted to be in the midst of the work, and how all of the above actually affected the quality of my work whether I knew it or not.

When I was at my lowest point, my *quality of experience* started to matter. In that moment, the *how* became just as important, if not more, than the *what*. I recognized that *the way* I worked had the potential to either energize or drain me. When I had the choice to drag myself over the finish line of some project late at night or get some rest and start it fresh first thing in the morning, I turned to the question of my quality of experience. Which would enable me to get it done with more joy? Which would enable me to bring excellence? Which would ensure that I'd be more willing to do it over and over again? Unless you are a vampire (and I know some of you are), perpetual all-nighters are just not sustainable. And even if your mind is not paying attention, you best believe that your body is keeping track.

Work as Safety, Security, Purpose, Community

When we consider all of the reasons why we trade so much of ourselves in the name of work, it really comes down to four fundamentals we expect the system of work to provide.

- We need to feel safe.
- We need to feel some sense of certainty and consistency.
- We need a sense of mission, meaning, and purpose.
- We need positive and affirming human connection in order to thrive.

In our traditional story of success, these concepts have been something that work has provided: pride, purpose, dignity, financial security, and belonging. There was a culture of loyalty that previous generations could rely upon when building a life and a career. And perhaps within that context, some of those sacrifices such as the long hours and the hard labor made sense.

But as the world of work has changed, particularly over the last 25 years, those deliverables have not only shifted, but have actually moved in the other direction. As the rising statistics on physical and emotional violence and toxicity grow, work has not been safe. As the volatility of our economy and the precarious nature of the free market has intensified, there has been greater uncertainty and inconsistency across the board all in the face of shareholder expectations for greater profits. As the relentless pivoting of organizational priorities occurs, diluted directives undermine any real sense of purpose, mission, or meaning. As organizational structures have either been held hostage by singular agendas or collapsed under the weight of all this pressure, the culture of human connection has been deprioritized—and professionalism has become code for practicing emotional distancing. Loyalty is not a word we hear much anymore when it comes to work because as companies and organizations battle to survive, they make choices every day that impact people's lives.

In the midst of these shifts, we've had to fight harder to maintain and survive. And even when we do, safety, security, purpose, and community at work are not only things we can no longer take for granted, they've in many ways become philosophically a luxury— hence our low expectations. The most acute pain we feel in our Negotiation is coming to terms with the fact that we can still painfully sacrifice and never truly achieve any of the above—whether we gain

25

Success as Sacrifice: An Unchallenged Story

all of the external trappings or not. Which of course then begs the question, *What is it all for?*

Our growing Resignation is asking tough questions. Questions like, In this era of work is the story of success that we've bought into even attainable? When I get there, wherever "there" is, will I really be happy? And most importantly, What will be the cost on me—mentally, spiritually, and emotionally when I have to face the accumulation of all that navigating in the face of my own lack of fulfillment? Worse still, what happens if I'm doing all of this sacrificing while someone else is blocking the door?

Your Terms

1. Write down the success story you started your career or job with; what did success look like to you back then?

2. As you think back on what you believed was necessary to achieve success, list the concessions—even the small, seemingly trivial ones—you've actually made along the way. This may not be the most fun exercise you've ever done, but never fear: We'll be learning how to channel these insights into greater motivation in the chapters ahead.

For more downloadable tools and resources, go to: www.move thecrowd.me/IA-resources.

Chapter 3

When Failure to Succeed Is Almost Guaranteed: Thwarting

"As a Black-bodied woman I was expected to toil. My hard work was nothing special—as compared to my white counterparts who would receive praise for the littlest things."

—Anonymous

Our faith in the success story is based on our belief that it is possible—for every single one of us—to reach the mountaintop. But that belief ignores the true nature of the terrain, because in fact all paths are *not* created equal. Our system of work has never been a meritocracy, nor is success a matter of individual achievement.

For some, the way is smoothly paved and well-lit, with abundant signposts and helpful guides just where you need them. For others, not only is the road unpaved, but it's full of detours, gaping potholes, giant boulders, occasional landslides, and such poor lighting that you sometimes can't even see where you are, let alone where you're going. Some of the people you come across *could* guide you but choose not to. Some of the people you come across actively want to trip you up. To add insult to injury, this road is a toll road, and often you can't afford the toll, metaphorically and sometimes literally.

This is what I call *thwarting*. And it happens to the best of us. My jaw still drops when I think about Nikole Hannah-Jones, who—despite having won a Pulitzer Prize, a MacArthur "Genius" grant, a Peabody Award, a National Magazine Award, a Knight Award for Public Service, a George Polk award, and too many other awards, honors, and accolades to include here—was offered the Knight Chair in Race and Investigative Journalism at the University of North Carolina but denied tenure, unlike every Knight Chair who came before her. Every Knight Chair who came before her was white. Hannah-Jones, the *New York Times* journalist whose 1619 Project centers American history on Black Americans, is Black.

Thwarting Feels Personal ... but It's Actually Systemic

To thwart is to oppose, intercept, usurp, and or derail someone's road to success because you believe they are undeserving. The most important universal characteristic of thwarting is that it feels as if it's personal. This is by design—"she doesn't like me," "he's out to get me," "they don't want to see me succeed"—but when you look at the data and the uncanny similarities among stories, it's as if there is a playbook for how to block and tackle a career. Those who set the standard are simply running those plays, in different contexts and industries over and over again.

How can this be? Just as our system of work carries an ethos around success, it also carries an expectation around *who* is supposed to succeed. And when those who set the standard see others rising who don't fit that profile, or who in some way don't represent what they know and are comfortable with, then all of a sudden the terrain (and the rules) start to change. The system starts to put on the breaks.

In her response to the Board of Trustees actions at UNC coming to light, Nikole Hannah-Jones issued a personal statement shared via the Legal Defense Fund that says it all:

> "The Board of Trustees wanted to send a message to me and others like me, and it did. I always tell college students and journalists who are worried that they will face discrimination, who fear that they will be judged not by their work but for who they are or what they choose to write about, that they can only worry about that which is in their own control: their own excellence. I tell them all they can do is work as hard as possible to make themselves undeniable. And yet, we have all seen that you can do everything to make yourself undeniable, and those in power can change the rules and attempt to deny you anyway."
>
> —Nicole Hannah Jones, Legal Defense Fund[1]

The Myth About Merit

In the story of success, we've been taught to believe that someone has become successful because they've worked really hard, possess certain qualities, or have demonstrated certain skills that make them "special," i.e. better suited than the rest of us to sit at the table. We've also been taught that their place in that coveted seat is in the best interest of the whole. That's the meritocracy argument. But you and I both know (or at least we are starting to recognize) that the story of success is plagued by other agendas. These agendas do not necessarily reflect merit or "the best interest of everyone involved"; in fact, there are entire systems and structures that are designed to ensure that the standard setters and those who do their bidding maintain that expectation of who should be at the top.

When Failure to Succeed Is Almost Guaranteed: Thwarting

I remember the first time I came across Mokgadi Caster Semenya; I'd purchased a magazine on running. I was so drawn to her image that I wanted to know her story. Caster is a South African elite middle-distance runner, a two-time Olympic champion, and a three-time World Champion who began competing on the international stage in 2008. After her electrifying win at the 2009 World Championships, she was required to undergo gender-based testing due to the presumption that her incredible performance in the 800-meter race raised suspicions about whether or not she was even a girl and if her elevated testosterone levels gave her an unfair competitive advantage over the other women athletes. In her unflinching autobiography, *The Race to Be Myself*, Caster brings to light the lived experiences of intersex discrimination in the world of elite sports. She describes the evasive way she was ushered into a series of intrusive "tests" that ultimately culminated in her needing to take medication to "suppress" her testosterone level in order to run. Even with all of the obstacles and the criticism, she considers herself to be fortunate when compared with other elite women runners who were, early in their careers, pressured into agreeing to genitalia-altering medical procedures. There was a moment in the sport where Caster recognized two important things: (1) that the rules (though presented as hard and fast) kept shifting, and (2) that there seemed to be an underlying perception around who should be dominating in the sport versus who was actually winning at the time. This unfulfilled expectation of who should dominate created a hostile environment that made it almost impossible for her to compete.

The thwarting 101 playbook on this reads as follows:

- **Step #1—Cast Doubt**—I have an assumption about what I believe a "woman" or a "champion" or a "tenured professor" should look like, and you're not it, so, I'm going to challenge your right to exist in this sport, on this stage, in this boardroom, in this role, at this company, etc. And not only am I going to challenge you but I'm going to create doubt in the minds of those around you and in the media, and among your peers, and other officials.

- **Step #2—Shift the Burden of Proof**—I'm going to couch it as *speculation* and then I'm going to put the burden of proof on you. Prove to me that you deserve to be here … prove to me that you are who you say you are, prove to me that you are not a liar and a cheat. And here's what you need to do in order to make me believe you … hurdle, hurdle, and even bigger hurdle.

- **Step #3—Change the Rules**—Yes, I know you thought x, y, and z were required when you were jumping all of those hurdles but now it's p, d, and q. Oh, and by the way, they need to be met under these very specific conditions that create the narrowest margin for success.

- **Step #4—Turn Up the Heat**—Leak private information, start rumors, challenge credibility, integrity, and identity, distract from the real issue, disrupt your (mental, financial, emotional) stability, try in the court of public opinion.

- **Step #5—Control The Narrative**—Craft the story to make it appear as if you're just "doing your job" and protecting the "sanctity" of the institution. Paint the unlikely candidate as a "rebel" and "outsider" who has come to break the rules and threaten the established order of things.

31

The most effective tool that thwarting uses is shaming—public humili-ation and alienation that destabilizes our most basic human needs—to belong and to feel safe. When someone comes for you, they're chal-lenging the very fabric of your identity—and in Caster's case they didn't just challenge her gender, they went after her humanity.

Thwarting is a form of violence because it disrupts your sense of trust—not only trust in others, but also trust in yourself which is the most painful part. In our society, we've been taught to believe that something that gets said over and over again *must* be true. Someone who is deemed to be powerful and respected (aka feared) raises an eyebrow at the mention of your name and suddenly everyone backs away. Thwarting wields the power of influence both real and perceived to get the "unlikely candidate" to bend to the will of the standard setter or to give up the pursuit altogether.

In the moving epilogue to her book, Caster shares, "I'm still fighting, so I'm not in peace, but I have made peace with whatever cross this is I have to bear. I'll never be in peace until I and every other woman like me can run free."

Who's in Charge?

One of the most disorienting things about thwarting is that it can almost feel like you're imagining things. Sometimes the antagonizer is clear, but many times, it's not. Sometimes the disruptions are bla-tant and sometimes they are subtle and elusive. Thwarting often operates in secret and in service to the established hierarchy. And it begins almost at the point of entry. There are gates and ceilings, walls and trap doors—triggers, warnings, and mechanisms that all operate to ensure that the table and all of the most viable seats remain firmly within the standard setters control. Standard setters, when in power, are charged with maintaining the status quo. They unapologetically make the rules, change the rules, and break the rules all in service to this commitment.

I first heard the term "pipeline problem", circa 1995 when the field of diversity (i.e. training initiatives on gender, orientation, and racial equity) was heating up. Yet again, consultants rallied for another opportunity to try to level the playing field. When organizations got cornered about their lack of gender, sexual orientation, and cultural representation, the go-to response was "limited talent pool"—aka the "there are just not enough qualified women, Latinx, LGBTQ+, fill-in-the-blank people to interview for the job" argument. This myth has been challenged, successfully I might add, for decades. Pick your field—tech, finance, engineering—and you will find that the educational pools for these fields among women and culturally diverse communities has grown *exponentially* over the last 25 years.

By the time we got to 2020, organizations were out of excuses. In the heat of a post-George-Floyd DEI surge, when a prominent CEO of a major bank said, "We just don't have the talent pool," all hell broke loose. We began to see all kinds of research flooding the market in an attempt to explain what was really going on. In McKinsey's famed 2018 report, "Delivering On Diversity," it clearly demonstrated that businesses with diverse teams financially out-performed homogeneous teams by 35 percent.[2] The data showed there was no pipeline issue in terms of entry; however, as careers aged for certain groups, the rate of advancement slowed almost to a halt. This shifted the narrative to "you might get in the door … but the degree to which you would rise, well, that was another matter."

From McKinsey and Lean In's 2022 report,[3] we all enter the workforce with roughly population-equivalent representation at the ground level;

When Failure to Succeed Is Almost Guaranteed: Thwarting

however, as time goes on, many of us don't rise. And it doesn't seem to matter what industry you choose; the data looks pretty similar for the same groups of people.

So what happens between the ground floor and the penthouse suite? It's a myriad of mazes and obstacle courses that continue to produce the same outcome over and over. In a staggering *New York Times* article titled "The Faces of Power: 80% Are White,"[4] a graphic topped the spread with a subtitle that read: "*These are 922 of the most powerful people in the United States. 180 of them identify as either Black, Hispanic, Asian, Native American or otherwise a person of color.*"

What made the article so groundbreaking wasn't just the color contrast of the visual. It was the acknowledgment that we often don't SEE the faces of those who call the shots. We see charts and bars, Venn diagrams and tables that give us the trends, but none of them really tell us who's in charge. This article was different because it humanized the challenge we are facing.

In our inherited definition of success, reaching the mountain top typically includes some perks like a corner office, an awesome assistant, an invitation to the executives lounge, and oh, yeah, having dominion over others. And it's that dominion part that will get you thwarted every time. Traditional power is rooted in visible and invisible human hierarchies that date back almost to the beginning of time. And granting the power to make decisions that affect others is not something that is ever taken lightly—certainly not by a standard setter. Who gets to succeed in any given context is directly connected to who those in power believe they have the ability to influence—for better or worse.

In many instances, no matter who ultimately sits in the seat, there are ingrained ways of operating that make it impossible for certain members of society to ever truly rise to any significant level of influence. And if they do, you'd better believe that the pressure to toe the line is almost unbearable. So even when it looks like there's new blood, there are structures and protocols that remain deeply ingrained and extend beyond whoever takes the chair.

These systems reinforce themselves over time through ingrained rituals and traditions, and they may never be scrutinized by those newly occupying the seat. Changing the identity of the person in the chair doesn't automatically usher in a new status quo. The "if it ain't broke, don't fix it mentality" or the "this is how we do things here" mantra prevails more than we'd ever like to admit.

Moreover, as much as we'd like to believe that systems are neutral and arbitrary, they are not. They discriminate based upon the nature of the ingrained structures, policies, and decision-making protocols that uphold them. Overthrowing a system on the big screen makes for an epic and thrilling story, while overthrowing systems in real life is far more arduous, perilous, and slow moving. In fact, the system can often rely on the sheer exhaustion of the individual and depletion of resources before it will ever experience a true threat—or so it may seem.

Thwarting Is Big Business

Thwarting doesn't just begin when we enter the "professional world." The wheels on the structures of inequity begin turning for many at the point of birth. And though we struggle to identify and capitalize on pipelines for advancement, when it comes to those unlikely candidates, we find tremendous flow in the pipelines that are designed to thwart their progress. These systems are insidious, far-reaching, and overwhelming in their effectiveness. And one doesn't have to go far to recognize the intergenerational effects on who gets to rise.

Robert K. Merton, who is considered to be a pioneering force in the field of sociology, has been a vital force in helping us understand the process of socialization. In addition to giving us the term "role model," he also coined the phrase "self-fulfilling prophecy."[5] A self-fulfilling prophecy is defined as the adoption of a false belief that influences one's behavior in a way that ultimately makes that belief come true.

The School to Prison pipeline advocates, like those at the Black Child Agenda[6] and the Anti-Defamation League,[7] draw on this theory to describe the phenomenon happening with poor, Black, disabled, and LGBTQ+ children in public schools. This pipeline theory describes how the perception of these children has influenced the dramatic shift in the punishments for offenses that would traditionally receive a trip to the Principal's Office or detention, now being met with suspension, expulsion, and even arrest. It asserts that these punishments push Black children out of schools and into the Juvenile Justice System. According to a Learning for Justice article[8] on the School to Prison pipeline, which cites a study conducted by the US Department of Education's Office for Civil Rights, Black students were 3.5 times more likely than white students to receive such harsh punishments like suspension and expulsion; students with disabilities were twice as likely to experience the same treatment.

Building on Merton's theory, social justice advocates like those at the *Law Journal for Social Justice*[9] uncovered that the underlying *economic* conditions of these students often set the stage for such severe (and unequal) treatment. This realization has evolved the School to Prison pipeline theory into the Poverty to Prison pipeline theory which describes the ways in which the United States punishes those who lack sufficient financial resources. This theory points to the direct correlation between race, poverty, and incarceration. The orchestrating and sustaining of economic instability has proven to be big business for standard setters who are committed to maintaining their praxis of power and control. There are narratives rooted in various forms of identity that feed thwarting. And the intersectionality of those identities and corresponding narratives can prove to be lethal when it comes to road blocking success.

When you perpetually deny people access to basic and fundamental human needs, force them outside of traditional systems of economic sufficiency by denying them a living wage, and then punish them for under-earning or earning outside of those traditional systems, you criminalize their right to survive. Moreover, when you then marginalize them further once they've "paid their debt" to society by forcing them back into those same under-earning positions, you perpetuate the cycle of poverty and criminalization. One only needs to observe the data to discover that pipelines of thwarting thrive on these distorted narratives and self-fulfilling prophecies rooted in low-income and underrepresented communities.

According to the *Law Journal for Social Justice*: "Incarcerated peoples' median income is less than $20,000 (a year) before incarceration, and this number is not only a result of the racial income gap. While 80 percent of the people incarcerated come from low-income communities, 67 percent are minorities. These numbers are clearly very close to each other and alarming, but they suggest that poverty is almost more determinative of whether or not a person will have contact with the prison system."[10]

According to a Prison Writers article titled "Educate Not Incarcerate,"[11] there are approximately 2.3 million people incarcerated (in the United States) at an average cost of about $36,000/year. An online college degree can be obtained for just $14,000. The data has proven that investments in education reduce rates of incarceration and recidivism and provide pathways for economic stability not only for our youth but for families too. Yet it has required massive efforts to implement educational programs within correctional institutions as well as to offer young people educational alternatives when they struggle within the current public school systems.

Systemic roadblocks are hard to pinpoint, but they feel like walls, career walls, life walls, relationship walls. They show up as never-ending cycles and loops, as generations of poverty and abuse, as glass ceilings, as violence and corruption, as economic and resource insecurity, as bureaucracy and red tape, and as hoops and hurdles that seem totally unreasonable yet are unequivocally required. These systems undermine what we believe and dictate how our organizations operate, how we treat one another, and even how we treat ourselves.

Whether we look through the lens of Academia, Sports, Corporate America, Primary Education, or Entertainment, we find a courageous assortment of outliers who've been willing to overcome unprecedented challenges and defy the odds to take their seat. But the story of success is incomplete without acknowledging the challenges that come with those chairs, not to mention the many more narratives of those who have tried valiantly to rise but who, through no fault of their own, have not been able to ascend. This is the cost of Negotiation, the stark realization that we are playing someone else's game. With fluctuating terms, on faulty terrain. And if your fate is left in *those* hands, then the odds of thriving are precarious at best, and nonexistent at worst. The system is always (for better or worse) going to choose its own survival, and if we don't become more intentional about our participation, then Resignation *is* the destination.

Your Terms

1. In what ways have you experienced, witnessed, or even participated in the practice of thwarting? Use this opportunity to witness your own experience and honor those feelings.

2. Share your journey with people you know, love, and trust. Allow your story to be a source of strength and empowerment.

For more downloadable tools and resources, go to: www.move thecrowd.me/IA-resources.

Part II

Resignation

As painful as it is, Negotiation (aka Navigation) is all we've ever known. No matter how big or small the concessions, the miles, feet, and inches do add up. The hard work, the painful sacrifice, the systemic road blocks—our job has been to navigate it all with the hopes of being able to be heroic and retire in 30 or 40 years. That's when we'll have the freedom to do what we want—in that "some-day" off in the distance. But 30 years is a long time to wait for … any-thing! Especially when it's never guaranteed.

Even with the advent of new industries that proclaim innovation, we're still seeing some of the same old systems at work because the definitions and expectations surrounding success remain the same. Resignation is a tricky thing; it can hide out in our comfort zones and packed agendas, it can show up as perfectionism and pragmatism, it can even masquerade as company Kool-Aid flavored ambition. In this part, I'll introduce you to the various shades of your own Resignation 1.0 *and* 2.0. We'll examine the unique threshold of your toleration—what it is and how it's been developed over time. And we'll confront the wounded nature of many of your greatest motiva-tions as you consider where you are now and where you want to go.

Chapter 4

One Coin, Two Sides: Giving Up vs. Quitting

"Mandated. Essential. Lack of Value—is pretty much how I felt when I (as a network engineer for the lottery) had to come into work when the world was dying."

—Anonymous

At some point, many of us come to accept that the idea of success we bought into is not going to happen. The game as it's currently designed is not winnable. The toxic culture of our workplace—favoritism, backstabbing, microaggressions, gaslighting, exclusion—isn't going to change. It is neither equitable nor inclusive. We feel apathy about our situation and don't see a way out. So, we give up—on the situation and, by extension, on ourselves. And in giving up, we enter the next phase on the continuum: We become resigned.

Some people—actually, a lot of people—reach this point of the continuum and stay there for the duration of their working lives.

Such was the case for a funny and gregarious friend I'll call Sam. Sam had an executive role at a midsize company with a high-stress, super demanding culture. The company *said* all the right things about its mission and values, but it rarely followed through. Big announcements about new work culture and employee-based initiatives were happening all the time, but three months later … crickets. The last time we spoke, the company had just gone through yet another reorganization that put even more on Sam's plate. When I pressed him about how bad it was on a scale of 1 to 10, he snorted and said, "Eleven." My usual bubbly friend looked exhausted, and I could tell he was doing everything he could to stay upright in his chair. Then he quipped, "But hey, it won't be forever, I'm gonna retire in seven years." I'm sad to admit that I immediately thought, *If you make it.*

Other people, feeling the same alienation and unhappiness, go from the Resignation 1.0 of *being* resigned—i.e., giving up—to actually *resigning*, what I call Resignation 2.0. When the workplace or the venture clearly won't work for them, they throw up their hands and say, "Peace out!" It usually happens at the point of a person's greatest awakening.

It might seem strange to you that Sam didn't quit, that he kept deciding to stay. But to me it was clear: As difficult as things were, Sam had not reached his *tolerance threshold*—the tipping point between what you can resign yourself to accepting and what is ultimately too much. Every person has such a point, and each person's threshold is unique.

There are many reasons why someone might have a high tolerance threshold. It could be their circumstances: economic insecurity, a temperamental need for stability, other people depending on them for support (financial, health insurance, etc.). It could be their psychological make-up and what they've had to endure, especially if they were taught to believe that toughing it out is a sign of strength. It could be the pressure—self-imposed or otherwise—to reach a certain milestone or to achieve (or defy) expectations. But one reason that is *very* common yet often unconscious or unacknowledged is the extent to which work has taken over our identities.

Just notice the way we tend to introduce ourselves. "I'm a real-estate agent," not "I sell houses." "I'm an architect," not "I design buildings." The distinctions might sound trivial, but the language reflects our reality. We put on the figurative uniform of our profession, go to work, and proceed to make concessions, contorting and erasing ourselves to fit the job. We hide or neglect or give short shrift to entire parts of our identity as though they don't matter, or even as though they're shameful. We forget that we're a whole person. And after a while the unconscious calculus is this: I have given so much to be here that I don't want to rock the boat. I have staked so much in order to get my *piece* that I can't afford to be disruptive, not even for the sake of my *peace*. I don't want to overthrow anything, I just want to be validated and accepted. I just want to be perceived as heroic. And so, we stay, resigned as in Resignation 1.0.

And our Resignation becomes most apparent as we approach our tolerance threshold. The closer we get, the more desperately we tend to engage in last-ditch efforts to make our situation work. Talk about negotiation! We furiously wheel and deal with ourselves in all kinds of (usually unspoken) bargains. On this side: our need to feel secure, our sense of duty or obligation, our longing to be accepted, our wish to look good to the world, our profound desire to not have to admit that we made a wrong move or were sold a bill of goods or stayed too long or are desperately unhappy. On the other side: our list of slights, grudges, and transgressions, our hurt feelings and sense of

45

One Coin, Two Sides: Giving Up vs. Quitting

being perpetually ignored or under attack—all adding up to our desperate unhappiness. We are at war with ourselves, and I can tell you from personal experience that most of us are inclined to hang on by the slimmest thread until we just ... finally ... can't.

In general, the state of our world breeds Resignation (the giving-up kind) and stasis (aka toleration). Our number-one agenda is to have comfort and safety. This mentality has taught many of us to put on blinders and just "trudge on through" as an ingrained response to chaos. There is a false belief that what happens "out there" doesn't affect us and that we can't affect it. But that belief has now been punctured. The events of recent history—#MeToo, Black Lives Matter, the murder of George Floyd, climate change, COVID, the attempts to subvert democracy—have popped the isolationist bubbles in which we thought we lived. On its own, one of these events, or even two or three, would likely not have been enough to provoke the mass awakening embodied in the Great Resignation. But their cumulative effect proved to be a force strong enough to overcome inertia on a massive scale. We saw that we're connected and mutually affected, and in that new light we saw ourselves differently. And many people realized they had to make a change.

What Did You Quit During the Pandemic?

When I asked Jose this question, he had to take a moment and think about it. A successful serial entrepreneur working in finance, his business exploded when the quarantine dropped into place.

> "Everybody wanted to do deals," he said. "And I was that guy! I found myself working almost around the clock to be able to keep up. My team couldn't hold the demand and so I had to step back into roles that I would traditionally

delegate." He paused. "And then I woke up one Saturday morning and my whole body felt as if it was on fire." He shifted uncomfortably in his seat. "I had to get to urgent care." There was a facility not too far from me, thank God. But remember, this is during the height of the pandemic and I had no idea what I might be walking into. They tested me for COVID, of course, but that came back negative. One nurse told me, "I think you have shingles."

"Sure enough, three days later, I had these raw, rash-like, red patches on my stomach that burned and itched like you would not believe." He looked me in the eyes. "Have you ever had shingles?" he asked. I shook my head "no." His skin flushed. "It was so bad, I couldn't even put on a shirt." He leaned forward. "Just imagine, having to be on Zoom calls, closing multi-million-dollar deals with high-pressure deadlines and feeling total agony every time I leaned forward and the fabric touched my skin." He scoffed. "Talk about brutal."

When I pressed him about why he got shingles in the first place, he chuckled and lightly scratched his head, "Musta been the stress." When I asked about his work ethic and what made him choose to work through it, he said, "You know, I was raised to believe that when it comes to work, you did whatever it took to get it done." He sat back. "But this experience, and how I felt as I dragged myself out of bed every morning, caused me to really look at my relationship to my health." He nodded, "The truth is, my health has always been a challenge for me—but this time ... this time was different."

One Coin, Two Sides: Giving Up vs. Quitting

How so? I asked, He sat quietly, taking in the question, then said, "I'm no longer willing to jeopardize my health for anything or anyone anymore."

For Alyssa, her departure was brought on by the imploding of her company. Like many organizations during the pandemic, her company was in the process of successfully digging themselves out when everything changed.

"It was utter chaos," she said. "The company went into this total financial free fall, I was having to fire-fight at every turn, people were burnt out, stretched beyond belief, and really scared about the future. Loyalties began to unravel, and I found myself having to consistently talk people off of the ledge." She shook her head. "I spent half my time trying to clean up rumors, half my time trying to get clear answers from leadership, and the other half of my time ... (notice I'm already at full time after the second half) trying to pivot to finding solutions." She ran her hands through her hair. "Then the layoffs started, tons of layoffs, every day. Can you imagine what it was like having those conversations, getting those emails from disgruntled former employees? I was beyond exhausted. And yet, I felt responsible for making sure that we did this right—that people were let go with some form of dignity." She sat back. "At some point I got really clear that it was not going to stop storming, this was the new normal and I just wasn't up for another eight months of being on the rollercoaster of economic uncertainty."

For Dane, it was an entirely different matter.

"I guess for me it came down to bullying," Dane said. "You know that saying, that people don't quit their companies, they quit their managers? Well, that was definitely my case." They paused. "I'd devoted the last five years to helping to make this family brand a household name and as much as they prided themselves on being a family culture, I can tell you it didn't feel like the kind of family I wanted to be in." They shook their head. "My manager constantly criticized, ranted, and raved about things that none of us could control, and then at some point it just got nasty." They frowned. "I remember receiving my final performance review, and he said, 'You know, I just don't think people like you.' Can you imagine? Someone in leadership saying that? Yea, I was done."

Traditional companies were not the only ones to experience this kind of fallout. People from all walks of life and occupations were struggling. There were the challenges of isolation that many felt who were sheltered in place as single people living far from home. There was the overwhelming majority of women with elderly parents and young children who were struggling, juggling the challenges of home care, schooling, caretaking, and working their own jobs all while trying to hold the emotional fabric of their families together. Then there were those on the frontlines who did not have the luxury of staying home. They had to get up and go to work every day and face a terrified and traumatized public, in warehouses, transportation centers, supermarkets, pharmacies, restaurants, hospitals, you name it, while the people around them were dying.

49

One Coin, Two Sides: Giving Up vs. Quitting

What We've Been Taught to Tolerate

In the United States, the story of success comes fully equipped with an ethos of rugged individualism. We've been told that truly successful people are totally self-reliant and self-made.

They are tough and resilient—unflinching in the face of challenge. In fact, the grin-and-bear-it mandate is so deeply ingrained in our culture that when you ask someone how they're doing, the automatic answer is "Fine!" regardless of what's really happening.

The challenge here is that when it comes to our mental, spiritual, and emotional well-being, there are so many fine lines that have to be untangled to determine what is a "character building experience" as my father would say versus what is just downright toxic. Many of us, given our experiences with childhood trauma or other forms of abuse, can't always tell where the line is, which makes it difficult to discern whether or not it's been crossed.

Just as we've developed strong narratives about success, we've also developed strong narratives about the perception of failing. "Nobody likes a quitter" we get told over and over again. Our inability to make it work becomes a personal indictment on our character implying we are lazy or incapable, that we are flawed, or somehow inadequate in the eyes of society and our peers. So we trudge on, even though we've *been* resigned.

In the spring of 2020, so many things came to a head—much of the world had just moved into sheltering in place, people were perishing at an alarming rate, businesses were scrambling, anxiety was at an all-time high, and then came the murders, culminating in the public lynching of George Floyd—and all hell broke loose. People poured into the streets, risking a deadly virus to protest injustice and force the hand of the system to "do something!"

As we witnessed these collective breaking points—each of us in our own right may have been navigating our own eruptions, not only in our workspaces, but on social media, in our larger communities, in the intimate relationships in our homes, and of course even within ourselves.

Through the limiting of our mobility, we were forced to be still and observe the truth of our own experiences. And in that examination, we started confronting where each of us may have been feeling powerless. What had we been avoiding? Where had we been careless and neglectful? Where had others been careless and neglectful with us? How much were we working? How well were we eating and sleeping? What kind of state were our most intimate relationships in? And where had we been planting roses on top of you-know-what?

Many of us had to confront the loss of loved ones. Many of us had to pivot to preserve our livelihoods. Many of us had to grapple with the political polarization around masking and vaxing within our own families—and the list goes on. Many of us had to own the degree to which we had been self-medicating and hence self-neglecting. And some of us had no idea what was truly important to us until that very thing was taken away. Above all, these breaking points and revelations drove home the simple fact that many of us had to face the fact that we weren't just stressed; we were in crisis.

These internal revelations fueled by the fire in the streets forced a kind of internal reckoning that awakened deeper questions about our humanity and who we really wanted to be vs. the role we'd been playing. In our state of Resignation, many of us gave up the quest to put up the facade as exhaustion, anxiety, and fatigue settled in. We came

One Coin, Two Sides: Giving Up vs. Quitting

to the Zoom call in sweaty t-shirts with unblurred backgrounds—no longer caring if the world saw what was really going on behind the scenes. We abandoned our "essential" jobs by throwing signs on the door that said, "Sorry, we quit!" The resistance to courageously facing our reality had finally hit the ultimate wall as our individual and collective thresholds of toleration got blown to smithereens.

And as much as we feel the pressure in this moment to go back to who we were and what it was before, it's just not happening. We are not the same. The (de) and (re) humanizing nature of what has occurred has shifted something deep within every single one of us and even if we can't quite put our finger on it—we know that *we* are changed.

Who Was, and Is Still, Quitting and Why?

Resignation in all forms is alive and well. We are in the throes of a universal breakdown and, dare I say, standoff with the traditional world of work. No amount of (low) funded initiatives, fancy press conferences, or tear-jerking commercials is going to sway us to return to the way it was. We are hip now—our eyes are wide open.

There have been so many "Greats" since our Resignation became known to the world. As much as we want to blame this ill-will on COVID and all of the events that have transpired during the last five years, it has been building long before our temperatures spiked. And the dissatisfaction just seems to keep growing.

We are searching for fulfillment, we want safety, we are looking to be valued, and we are hungry for growth, investment, purpose, and meaning. The traumatic and awakening experiences of the last five years have caused us to want *more*, not just in the quantitative sense but in the quality of our lives and day to day experiences. We want a greater quality of work.

A 2023, Microsoft/LinkedIn study states that "59% of U.S. job seekers feel stuck in their current roles. 51% are burned out from their jobs. And globally, that 68% (of workers) struggle with the pace and volume of work, and 46% feel burned out."

We keep hitting that career aka life wall because there is a fundamental disconnect between the expectations of organizations and their contributors that is perpetuating this divide. All attempts at purporting business as usual seem to be failing. But some would also argue that even new well-intentioned employee-based initiatives don't seem to be faring any better, so what are we missing? I believe there is a lack of shared understanding about the changes we've been through on all sides, and this lack of understanding will have deep and far-reaching implications on our individual and collective futures.

Because trust in the system and the process of work has been broken on such a fundamental level, many of us are no longer buying into the traditional story of success as *our* story. Therefore, the current construct of work isn't working—because it hasn't even considered the possibility of a new definition—one where more people can thrive and prosper. The takeaway on our Resignation resides in a fundamental us-versus-them, zero-sum mentality that continues to purport that the system works only when the majority of us are exploited.

So who's still quitting?

Gen Z grappled mightily with isolation and anxiety during the pandemic. They've also struggled with the strict cultural mandates of "professionalism" that have challenged their ability to foster authentic human connection which has in turn challenged their ability to

53

One Coin, Two Sides: Giving Up vs. Quitting

build trust. If we combine the isolation with rigid social norms, long hours, and less than inspiring work—you might find the recipe for their dissatisfaction.[1]

During the pandemic women faced a myriad of challenges because they held the brunt of the caretaking responsibility. All of this in the face of navigating their own hurdles; including but not limited to gender politics, hostile work environments, mental and emotional strain, physical burnout, and fatigue. Stretching to meet all of the expectations pushed millions to the breaking point—hence their mass exodus from the workplace all together in 2022. (BTW—according to the US Chamber of Commerce, 617,000 women have yet to come back.)

The outlook for essential workers doesn't look much better. An eye-opening article by the HR Platform Beekeeper in January 2023, titled "The Real Reason Why Your Frontline Workers Are Quitting,"[2] found that the challenges faced for frontline workers are even more severe. There are massive shortages of contributors from quiet quitting, absenteeism, and ghosting. Low wages, inadequate training, understaffing, malfunctioning of key equipment, and workplace safety have all made the list to help justify the current state.[3]

The Distance Between Quitting and Giving Up

The distance between quitting and giving up is oh so short but yet so far. How do you know when you've had enough? What are the signs in your mind, body, and spirit that tell you "*no mas!?*" What are the situations and circumstances that enable you to take a stand when for years you've been laying down? As we enter this new phase of enlightened Resignation, each of us must examine where that line is and how that line has evolved over the last five years.

As we dig through all of the layers of our experience and settle into the quiet of our own truth, we'll want to ask ourselves—where have I crossed my tolerance threshold? And where might I still be holding on? Because even when the story of success delivers, there's still a price (toll) involved.

Your Terms

1. Can you identify any place in your life or work where you've reached your threshold of tolerance? What do you notice about the choices you're making in that area?

2. If you've chosen Resignation 1.0 (i.e. to stick it out), what have been the most crucial factors that have influenced your decision? If you've chosen Resignation 2.0, what has it been like for you to ultimately let go? Are there any lingering regrets or challenges? Have there been celebrations or new insights?

3. How has your threshold of tolerance changed in the last five years?

For more downloadable tools and resources, go to www.move thecrowd.me/IA-resources.

55

One Coin, Two Sides: Giving Up vs. Quitting

The Suck in Success

"Success is a double-edged sword, it breeds an urgency... when you become a hit, you say, 'Oh, I have everything I want. No, wait, I want more'—to what end?"

—BB, Author, Millennial Entrepreneur

Our Resignation doesn't only live in our failures. Many of us are immersed in Negotiating when navigating the challenges of our successes too. On some levels, success can sometimes seem worse: you imagine the thing, you strive for it, you achieve it, and then that's when the real headaches start!

Can you hear Biggie Smalls ("Mo' Money Mo' Problems") or Jay-Z's ("99 Problems") bumping in the background? For my non hip-hoppers, allow me to translate: being successful is *stressful!*

You may look fabulous on the red carpet, but sometimes you will discover that all that glitters is not gold.

The Suck in Entrepreneurship

What happens when you're doing your dream job and you're still miserable? Extra misery, that's what! Unhappiness when you're doing work that you're genuinely aligned with is especially disorienting because the cognitive dissonance can be so great. I know, because this is what happened to me.

It is December 28, 2017, and I have just hung up the phone with my finance team. Every 12 months we review the scoreboard and debrief the results. This year, the results are impressive: record sales, exciting new partnerships and projects, phenomenal impact among those we served. On the surface it all looks good … but I am not good.

I am tired, I am angry, and I'm disappointed. As much as I should be celebrating, kicking back, and taking it easy, I'm still working. This one needs that, that one needs this, so and so is not responding to so and so, and they need me to intervene. Real talk? I want to douse my business in gasoline and set the whole thing on fire. I used to love this work, so what the hell happened? How did I go from being euphoric to being miserable?

At what point did my dream become my nightmare?

On that fateful evening in 2017 I learned a very hard lesson about success: everything you want may not be good for you.

As I turned to dissect the origins of my misery, I discovered a patch-work quilt of functional dysfunction informed by incidents from my childhood that I had buried deep. That, along with a romanticized hustle-grind ethos, kept me stuck in a never-ending loop of over-promising and under-delivering to the people who mattered most.

On paper, I looked amazing, but the truth was, I was a hot mess. I was working almost 20 hours a day, constantly on call, mediating drama between team members, cleaning up mistake after mistake, all while trying to keep my beloved clients and partners happy, healthy, and on track for achieving their goals.

Somewhere along the way I became a total prisoner to my quest for success. Even in charting success "on my own terms" I'd become a slave to some image I had conjured up about how it was supposed to look and who I was supposed to be in the midst of it all. My vision and commitment to holding space for world transformation in every facet of my life was giving me a headache.

How the hell did I get here?

"Here" doesn't just happen all of a sudden. It is a slow and sometimes invisible succession of moments that take us further from our truth. As entrepreneurs, in the Negotiation phase, every day we're making conscious and unconscious decisions. Then one day, we arrive at that place where our choices catch up to us and we just can't fake it anymore.

When I got to the bottom of my own mental breakdown aka Resignation, I was humbled to discover all of the things that were driving me. The company was in a growth spurt, and I felt it was my job personally to lean in and expand the company. I was passionate about our mission and saw the potential to take our impact to a whole new level. The more things we took on, the harder I worked.

In the midst of it all I'd gotten completely bogged down. I was stretched way beyond anything sustainable and totally consumed with trying to bring this vision for growth to life. What I would come to understand later with the help of an amazing therapist and my beloved coach, Barbara, was that I was actually in the midst of a full-blown series of trauma-triggered responses that were activated by the death of my father who passed away at the end of the previous year. My father was my world and the reason I pushed myself so hard to succeed.

Totally unbeknownst to me, I dissociated so that I could get through it all. After he passed, I threw myself full force into my work without taking a breath to really mourn or grieve. It wasn't until I battled through a racialized firestorm within my team that came to a head around the protests in Charlottesville, Virginia, in the summer of 2017 that I began to realize that I was not okay.

The strain of life, work, and world all came crashing down around me and by the end of 2017, I literally could not get off the couch. Little did I know I would see this same pattern repeat itself out in the world.

The Trauma in Success

In October 2017, while I was in the midst of my own unraveling, iconic women in Hollywood began to speak out about their experiences of sexual harassment and assault at the hands of a number of very powerful and prominent men. The #MeToo movement, going back to 2006 when it was founded by sexual assault activist Tarana Burke, took on a whole new dimension as celebrities started coming forward to courageously tell their stories and focus a spotlight on the realities of millions of professional women around the world through the hashtag #MeToo. Though the movement was rooted in sexual abuse and harassment, it opened an important doorway to the conversation of trauma and, more specifically, trauma related to professional success.

Of course we'd always known that sexual harassment existed in the workplace, but these accounts were so egregious and pervasive that many of us challenged how far we'd really come as women in our quest for equality. And it threw into question whether this kind of harassment and abuse had simply become an accepted rite of passage for any woman with a dream and the drive to pursue it.

As I watched the almost daily reveals, I asked myself what had these women endured in order to take those seats of power and influence. That in turn forced me to confront all of the places where #Ihaddone-ittoo! That led me to ask myself: What *is it about the nature of our aspirations that causes us to tolerate hostility and abuse as part of the natural order of getting ahead?*

Just as I began going deep on this question, I saw the brave testimony of Terry Crews in June 2018. Crews, a former NFL player turned author, actor, and advocate, was at a dinner party, a star-studded affair when he was cornered by a powerful male agent who groped his crotch. When asked during his testimony before a Senate Judiciary Committee, why he, a married, muscle-bound man who stood at 6'2" and weighed 245 pounds did not resort to violence, I will never forget his words, "Senator, as a Black man in America," he paused struggling to compose himself.

"Say it as it is," Senator Feinstein encouraged.

"You only have a few shots; you only have a few chances to make yourself a viable member of the community. I'm from Flint, Michigan, and I've seen many Black men who have been provoked and they've ended up in prison or dead. I am thankful to my wife because she prepared me. She said if you ever get goaded, do not respond … she trained me. It was because of the strength of my wife … the training worked."[1]

#MeToo was not just about an isolated group of women (and several men) standing up to courageously tell their stories. It pointed to something far more sinister and insidious in our culture, which is the expectation that success requires a kind of sacrifice that goes far beyond hard work. Success demands that we trade *flesh*—vital pieces of ourselves in order to arrive at and eat from its table.

This kind of debilitating sacrifice isn't just painful, it's traumatic. But far worse is the ingrained expectation that enduring this kind of dehumanization is vital to our ascension, as is the cultivation of a capacity to block it out—*especially* when it's happening to us.

Let's be honest, we were not shocked by what happened with the events of #MeToo. Nor are we surprised by all of the people who witnessed these acts for years and did nothing. What ultimately had us in awe was the fact that these prominent icons were finally willing to risk everything to step into the light and talk about it.

What Happens When Superhumans Resign?

The difference between challenge and trauma is hard for many of us to see—particularly when we appear to everyone else to be on top of our game. Naomi Osaka's culture-shifting *Time* magazine article in June 2021, "It's O.K. to Not Be O.K.," opened the door for challenging the long-standing "suck it up" code among professional athletes.[2]

When we think of any professional sport, we accept the fact that the training and competition are mentally, physically, and emotionally grueling. We even know that the greatest obstacles many athletes face happen off the court. Public scrutiny, blatant discrimination, even rampant cases of sexual abuse and assault have all been par for the course. But in this game-changing stance, Osaka unapologetically bucked the status quo by prioritizing her mental health and pressing pause on the constant pressures of being scrutinized in the press. This fierce solo act opened the door for a whole new dialogue around our often superhuman and sometimes inhumane expectations of athletes (and celebrities). Osaka stated, "There can be moments for any of us where we are dealing with issues behind the scenes. Each of us as humans is going through something on some level."[3] Soon after, she chose to step away to care for her mental health. In 2023, she became a mother and has recently returned to the 2024 US Open to upset Jelena Ostapenko in Round 1.

Simone Biles found that same courage when she pulled out in the final rounds at the Tokyo Olympics in September of that same year to focus on her mental health after experiencing immense pressure that triggered a condition in gymnastics called the "twisties," where a gymnast loses their bearings in midair. Biles stepped back because the experience heightened her concern about the risk of injury.[4] Biles took two years off and returned in the late summer of 2023 stronger than ever winning two golds and one silver at the World Championships and going on to win an additional three gold and one silver at the 2024 Olympics.[5] She retires as the most decorated gymnast in history with a total of 41 medals, 11 Olympic, and 30 Worlds—oh yeah, and she's the youngest person to receive the President's Medal of Honor too.

Then there's John Jaso who didn't just resign temporarily; he quit baseball all together—to go sailing! Jaso was a Major League Baseball player who walked away from it all. Even before he knew how to sail. Now, if anyone is living the dream, you'd think it would be a professional male athlete, adored by fans, making millions to play a game. But remember, each of us has a tolerance threshold, and everyone's threshold is different. Jaso had been traded multiple times, injured multiple times, but most crucially, *never felt like Major League Baseball was really him*—so he quit.

For Jaso, it came down to a lack of values alignment and the money was just not enough. "Even when I retired, people said: 'You might be walking away from millions of dollars!' But I'd already made millions of dollars. Why do we always have to have more, more, more?"[6]

The Truth Lies In Your Energy

These brave (coming out) stories don't just speak to the strength of these incredibly talented and capable individuals; they also speak to an oppressive competitive culture of success that has the propensity to push promising talent far beyond the limits of what should be acceptable in any profession. These grinding expectations wreak a kind of mental, physical, and emotional havoc that lingers long after the spotlight fades. What is it that we lose sight of in the pursuit that has us literally put our life forces at risk? The appearance of success is the allure but the reality of success for many exacts a price. Osaka says it all: "The intention was never to inspire revolt, but rather to look critically at our workplace and ask if we can do better."

As more athletes, entertainers, elite entrepreneurs, and leaders find the courage to come forward about the choice to step back to make the shift from being resigned about the nature of their success to resigning to reclaim their lives, and prioritize their well-being, they are sending us a wake-up call. Each of us has an opportunity to look more deeply at our own energy. Contrary to what we've been taught, your energy doesn't lie. If you're "successful" *and* exhausted, you might want to examine what's fueling your ambition.

Your Terms

1. As an energy-tracker exercise, consider which aspects of your life are feeding you?

2. Which ones are sucking you dry?

3. And, what's the rationale you're giving yourself in order to keep tolerating your current situation?

4. In the process, see if you can determine which form of resignation you may be in or moving through. Trust me: The results can be quite eye-opening.

For more downloadable tools and resources, go to: www.movethecrowd.me/IA-resources.

Chapter 6

Wounded Ambitions and Wounding Ambition

"My expectations of myself were always higher—I was like a machine, so much that I trained myself—I didn't even go to the bathroom during work hours—it was like a sickness."

—Anonymous

In the early days of my work as a soul coach, there was a lot of talk about purpose-driven anxiety. People were feeling a lot of stress because they didn't know what they wanted yet felt like they should. It turned out that the problem wasn't a lack of clarity about what they wanted, but a lack of *belief* that what they wanted was *valid*. This is a major factor for many people who stay in the Resignation (as in giving up) phase; they've learned not to value their own desires.

It begins when we first hear the word "no." If we're lucky, "no" arises in limited, reasonable circumstances, like when we're about to pull the dog's tail or run out into the street. Unfortunately, we often hear "no" simply because our desires conflict with someone else's—or with their perception of what our desires *should* be. As a result, many of us grow up tempering our desires to ensure that the people around us, the people in charge of us, feel pleased, comfortable, and in control. Depending on our upbringing, we may get even deeper cultural and institutional messages. If we're raised in a religious context to believe that we were born in sin, for example, then we are also often taught that our desires are unholy.

As we venture into the world, we receive similar reinforcing messages that suggest our wanting needs to be curtailed, especially when it comes to wanting for ourselves. Wanting to do the things that make us happy is often framed as being childish, selfish, and immature. "Grow up," we're told, or "Get real."

Depending on who you are and what you desire, wanting can be unacceptable, even dangerous. For example, when it comes to achieving big dreams and goals, people in marginalized groups are often told they're lucky to get anything at all. So fearing failure, trouble, ridicule, or ostracism, we distance ourselves from our deepest longings and start wanting what we're "supposed to"—the things that "make sense" or the things that align with what makes us "valuable" in the eyes of the powerful. This is what I call *wounded* ambition. It comes from a place of believing that who we are and what we want are not enough.

But then we look around and see that some people don't care about "supposed to." They defy the "no"s. And sometimes these people are *heralded* for their defiance. So, we ask ourselves: How come they get to buck the system and I don't? How come they get to be who they want and I don't? These questions generate anger and confusion. Our perception of a lack of fairness breeds an even greater sense of wounding and Resignation (1.0 *and* 2.0.).

Our wanting is complicated by another kind of wanting not in the sense of desire but in the sense of drive and the need for validation. Those of us who are driven to seek a stamp of approval are often people who lack a sense of our own value. We strive to feel worthwhile, and there can be a kind of desperation and aggression in this striving—exactly the kind of desperate, aggressive competition that our work culture tends to foster and reward. This is what I call *wounding* ambition. It also comes from a place of believing that *there is not enough* and that in order to ensure that we aren't left out, we may need to resort to doing things that take us outside of *how* we want to be—especially when it comes to the way we treat ourselves and others.

Five Types of Wounded/Wounding

In my experience of working with thousands of people, I've seen five types of wounding that can serve as massive drivers of our ambition.

- Imposter syndrome
- Righteous competition
- Lack of ownership/disenfranchisement
- Playing safe/small
- Hiding out

Whether we are desiring (wanting) on behalf of someone else's definition of success or whether we are pursuing (driving) in ways that perpetuate "not enough," these internalized wounds can influence our motivations and distort our perceptions about what success actually is and what is truly required in order to achieve it.

> I remember getting to know an entrepreneur I met at a retreat some years ago. We'll call him Steve. Steve was a rock star, no doubt. He was building a clothing line, he was developing a series of haircare and shaving products for men, he was building out a cool brick and mortar concept for stores he hoped to ultimately franchise—I mean the

vision was BIG and it was all very inspiring and exciting. After spending a couple of days with him—I noticed that he never stopped. He never stopped moving, never stopped talking, he never stopped hustling.

He'd fully embraced the lifestyle of being on-the-go and seemed to feed off of the adrenaline of moving from one thing to the next. But as I continued to engage with him, I began to notice that he became very short-tempered. He'd show up late to important meetings or sometimes not at all with a quick cryptic text hours later about getting caught up. He stopped saying please and thank you and started saying things like "I need this" and "you can do this for me, right?"

I'm not sure how long it took me, but at some point I became less enthusiastic about the venture, less amped up to receive his calls, less inspired to go out of my way. And I started to get reports from other contacts—incredible businesspeople who could help him—who were beginning to feel the same way, and they too started to back away. Each of us felt a sense of loss because we all knew that at the core of it all he was really a good guy and his vision was compelling. But he was consumed by something we couldn't fully understand that didn't seem to be leading him in a positive direction.

In our culture, we tend to revere this kind of drive—we overlook the slights because we just know that one day, this guy's gonna be famous and we want to be on the "ins" with him vs. on the "outs." We minimize the importance of the means because after all we are taught that they always justify the ends. But when the ends come to the detriment of everything else—you have to begin to question, *What is all of this striving really about?*

Intentional Ambition

Wounding #1: Imposter Syndrome

All of us pretend in some way. It is baked into our cultural norms and organizational procedures. It's ingrained in our upbringing and woven into the rituals of our daily interactions. Whether we smile when our heart is breaking or compliment a colleague who we cannot stand on a great presentation, these surface interactions represent the facade we wear and corresponding expectations that govern our behavior.

In fact, when we enter any environment, we are handed a set of social cues that tell us exactly where the boundaries lie. The subtle and not so subtle guidance we feel when we enter a room lets us know where the dos and don'ts reside. If we are good at reading and sensing, we can easily fall in line, and if we ever feel unsure, we all know that the appropriate response is to do nothing. Better to blend in and be forgotten than be remembered for making a mistake.

The term Imposter Syndrome was coined by Pauline Clance in her 1986 book, the *Imposter Phenomenon: Overcoming The Fear That Haunts Your Success*. In it she refers to a psychological state where one is unable to internalize their accomplishments and thus constantly feels like a "fraud."

I define it as an inability to see yourself internally *and* externally. Internally it manifests as the belief that when it comes to meeting the mark, you still have a long way to go. That your accomplishments, no matter what they are, don't count. Externally, it manifests as the absence of seeing someone who you perceive to be like you achieving at a high level. You question not only whether or not it's possible, but also if you even belong.

There are two aspects to this syndrome that are important to name. The first is the almost constant obsession with perfection, and the second is the recognition of the desire and drive to prove oneself. In our PowHer Redefined[1] research we found that 70 percent of the almost 1,800 women we interviewed stated that they felt the need to constantly prove themselves "over and over, and over, and over, again." Whether we are proving to ourselves we are capable or proving to others that they were wrong about us, the commitment to perfection creates a persona that is always reaching, striving, pushing, grasping as well as pleasing, appeasing, and deferring.

Our inability to see ourselves and our inherent value has very real consequences, especially if we get good at "being perfect." The gap between our true self and the facade we erect becomes so wide that *we* actually start to become disoriented, unsure even to ourselves of who is really in there. At some point, the toll becomes too great, the rewards too few, and ultimately we get tired of pretending. The unsustainable and debilitating nature of proving "perfection" has no choice but to lead to our Resignation.

Wound #2: Righteous Competition

The competitive nature of our world is unavoidable. Whether we like it or not, we are constantly enmeshed in some kind of comparison. Whether it's the not so harmless family dynamics among our parents and siblings or the not so subliminal messages we receive from the accolades that get handed out in our professional world, we all recognize that the standard of success is never without its trusty ruler that is constantly assessing whether we measure up.

Within our modern world, we are taught from the beginning that our job is to either pursue or protect our status. This is often determined by the mix of biological, cultural, geographical, and social factors and how each contributes to where we may stand on any given day. Within the social order systems there is the perception that you can trade up or down based upon certain factors, which include but are not limited to, intelligence, physical prowess, talent and ability, material resources, moral fortitude, beauty, race, class, gender, etc. When in the possession of these qualities, it is believed that society looks favorably upon you. You receive credibility, respect, trust, access, when you are on the "right" side of these equations. The possession of these "rights" is what gives you the ability to broker greater access and opportunity, especially when it comes to the world of business.

Alex is a bright young sales representative; he's handsome, charming, and *very* likable. From the onset of his eight-year career, he's been labeled as a rock star. He walks around the office in his tailor-made suits and designer watches looking and smelling like heaven. ALL of the ladies love him, and his clients just keep piling on the business. He's only got one real challenge: "I hate to lose," he says, "and I'll do just about anything to make sure I don't." He pauses, adjusting his posture, "But as I've grown, I have to admit, I've done some things that I regret." He continues, "There was this new sales rep a few years ago; she was really strong, and all of the managers started teasing me about not letting her outperform me. They said it as a joke, you know," he sighed. "But there's a part of me that really got riled up. I started to antagonize her—you know, to throw her off her game. If we had to make a presentation together, I'd withhold information, I'd cut her off when she was speaking, I'd give her a hard time anytime we got partnered up. At some point I think she just got fed up and quit."

Wounded Ambitions and Wounding Ambition

"After she left, the managers talked all this smack about how she just wasn't cut out for the role, you know, didn't mesh with the culture, but that was just crap. I drove her out."

The fight to be "right" is a cornerstone of wounded ambition. In the world of dominant power, being "right" entitles you to all sorts of things, including the "right" to challenge and demoralize those who are perceived to be your rivals (or beneath you).

But equal to the imposter, the righteous also battle with the exhaustion of having to perpetually make the case for (i.e. pursue or protect) why we deserve to move to the head of the line, why we have the right to judge, punish, and ostracize (or demonize) others. Moreover, right is always relative, meaning we can be right today and wrong tomorrow—on top one minute then rapidly declining the next.

The consequences of less than righteous tactics force us to reckon with where we've caused harm in the name of maintaining our lead or in getting ahead. The guilt we often carry feeds our Resignation when we ascribe to the belief that in order for us to progress we must be relentless and someone else always needs to be held back or pushed down.

Wound #3: Lack of Ownership/Disenfranchisement

When it comes to the pursuit of success, we get lots of mixed messages. Be bold and aggressive; no, be humble and patient. Be kind and generous; no, be selfish and egotistical. Follow the rules; no, break the rules. No, better yet, make the rules! I think you get it. In the arsenal of tactics for how we move ahead, lack of ownership/ disenfranchisement is a potent strategy because it operates on a conscious and subconscious level—with a rejection of vulnerability and transparency at the core.

When it operates subconsciously, it shows up as self-denial. You downplay your true desires ("who, me?") while trying to manipulate the circumstances in your favor. Common behaviors associated with lack of ownership are self-depreciation, passive aggressiveness, or back channeling; dropping those not so subtle hints about what you want while pretending it was someone else's idea—all to advance your desires.

When it's operating consciously, it shows up as denying others by standing in the way of their wants, needs, and desires. Common behaviors are classic thwarting in forms of gossip, gatekeeping, ostracizing, and scapegoating.

In both aspects, the end result is a lack of accountability, authenticity, and responsibility for your desires, choices, and behaviors.

Micia is a brilliant editor in constant demand. She's shy, friendly, and secretly very ambitious.

When people praise her, she deflects, "Oh, it wasn't that hard" or "You didn't really need me."

When a recent promotion opportunity came up in her division, she went to her boss to advocate for another member of her team. When he asked, "What about you?" Her response was, "Don't be silly … I could never do that job." Two weeks later, when the promotion was announced, Micia was furious. Storming into her boss's office holding up the announcement she asked him, "Really??" He stared back confused, "I thought you were behind this person. Didn't you come to me advocating for them?" Micia shook her head in frustration, "We all know that he's an idiot! When I came to you, you were supposed to talk me out of it and tell me to put my hat in the ring!" she bellowed. "Wait," her boss asked, "You wanted this position?" Flushed with rage she responded "DUH!"

Lack of ownership shows up prominently with people who were raised to be very competitive but who have never really felt like they had the permission to explicitly go for what they want. Disenfranchisement shows up with people who feel a sense of scarcity (or entitlement) around their status or position and who thwart in order to protect (the sanctity) what's "theirs."

This aspect of wounding has supported the rise of many (unsuspectedly) influential people. But the cost of disenfranchising is high—whether you do it to yourself or to another—because at some point you face the dilemma of credibility. Either your tactics run their course and become ineffective over time or you get found out and ultimately have to face the music. There will come a point of reckoning and the Resignation that follows can result in shame, grief, embarrassment, and even persecution.

Wound #4: Playing Safe/Playing Small

We love to be comfortable, even in our dysfunction. The devil we know is always better than the one we can't read. One of the biggest challenges with wanting is that you run the risk of being disappointed. And just as many of us have been conditioned to avoid disappointing others, we've been equally conditioned to avoid disappointing ourselves. This two-sides-same-coin phenomenon brings me to the wounded strategy of playing it safe while playing small.

Doing what comes easy rather than what feels exciting (the job, project, or task, etc.) may feel great in the beginning, but after a while, the restlessness kicks in. The drive to look good and the need to always be in control begins to feel hollow. Coasting eventually feels boring and even burdensome. And if you stay confined, the Resignation and resentment start to grow.

As much as we want a sure shot, many of us aspire to be challenged. We want and need critical feedback and work that has purpose and meaning. When we skate our way to "success," we rob ourselves of the opportunity to really discover what we're capable of and the actual difference we can make. Take a moment and consider how many people you know who are doing work that they're good at but have absolutely zero passion or challenge involved and you will begin to grasp just how pervasive this wound is. This is a major source of our Resignation—being under-engaged and underutilized.

Wound #5: Hiding Out

Behind every great visionary, artist, titan, president, etc., is someone who is avoiding their call; choosing instead to be the wind beneath someone else's wings. This person is incredibly capable, has a ton to offer, is vital to any operation, but runs from the spotlight or any form of attention. They hang back in the shadows because this is their comfort zone. They defer by nature, because they've been taught that if you want to get ahead, put everyone else first.

Kindred to those who play it safe, we stand back—never really challenging ourselves to secure a starring role in our own movie. We believe that everyone else is better, more equipped to deliver than we are. Yet, when game time comes, we're the ones calling the plays, designing the props, and leading the team to victory. We are uncomfortable with praise, yet we crave it. We work hard to make ourselves invisible yet resent being overlooked. We inherently know our value but feel frustrated when others don't see it. And as much as we have beef (i.e. issues) with our colleagues, we have much bigger challenges with ourselves.

Our justification for hiding stems from a deeply seeded fear that it's not okay to shine because shining doesn't just make you selfish, it makes you a target. So we work really hard, we keep our noses clean and our heads down, hoping and praying that someone will notice just how much of a gem we are—and convince us to finally step forward and lead.

But the consequences of being in a prolonged state where you feel overburdened and under acknowledged is a classic recipe for Resignation. Being "the glue" can give you a sense of purpose at the start, but it can quickly turn into burnout and the kind of exhaustion that is not easy to recover from.

When it comes to our ambition, these five wounded/wounding strategies are everywhere. Even with the best intentions, we can find ourselves resorting to choices and behaviors that compromise our values and disrupt our peace. Exploring our motivations can be tricky because our discoveries have the potential to challenge who we think we are and what we really value. Confronting the nature of our ambition is much less about what we say out loud and more about what we actually believe, think, feel, and do, especially when we're under pressure. The Resignation we feel when at the mercy of any one of these wounding strategies lets us know that we have veered away from our own happiness, joy, and fulfillment either in what we've reached for or in how we've reached. The most important part of our awakening and subsequent Renegotiating is to determine how we make our way back.

Your Terms

1. Take an inventory—notice which aspect(s) resonate most. Even if your own motivations don't always seem clear, you have certainly observed these motivations at play among others. Use those insights to dig deep into your own choices and responses.

2. When you consider what has fueled your own ambition is there any place where you've not felt the freedom to pursue what you wanted? Are you striving to meet someone else's expectations right now?

3. Is there any part of you that believes that an integral part of your pursuit will require you to do things that challenge or question your values? Why or why not?

For more downloadable tools and resources go to: www.move thecrowd.me/IA-resources.

Part III

Renegotiation

No matter how lofty it sounds, waking up is not easy. It can be daunting to challenge everything you've ever known in exchange for stepping into the *unknown*. Sometimes, we awaken with a gentle kiss, while other times we can be brutally punched in the chest. The pain, anger, and disorientation that can come with being thrust into the here and now are not uncommon. Similar to the stages of grief, we may find that there are layers upon layers of unexplored emotions and experiences that we need to process in order to arrive fully (i.e., back into our bodies, minds, and spirits).

There are times when Negotiation aka Navigation may have been useful to us, times when Resignation 1.0 was what kept the lights on. But when we enter Resignation 2.0, it gets real because we experience a moment of stark clarity connected to the realization of what we *don't* want. That, in turn, fuels our exodus from the status quo. When we finally find the strength to let go, we can feel really proud, excited, and amped up. But as we turn to face the uncertainty of our new reality, we can feel as if we're lost or in limbo—staring out into the abyss like "Now what?"

This is where we enter into the phase of Renegotiation. As much as the phases of Negotiation and Resignation may have been challenging and painful, there is no way you could have arrived here without them. The wisdom and insight you now have will serve you well, if those experiences can be placed into proper perspective. Renegotiation begins the moment you decide that who you've been, what you've done, what you've endured is no longer an option. It starts the moment you are truly ready to move forward. It begins with getting profoundly clear about who you are and what you want. It begins with telling the truth to yourself about what really matters.

Renegotiation is the place where you heal, transform, and restore. It's the place where you develop new aspirations along with new terms and conditions for how you'll show up and contribute. It's the place where you get to *Reclaim, Realign,* and *Reimagine.*

Chapter 7

Reclaiming: Whose Story Is It, Anyway?

"Going within has the potential to at the beginning and at the end bring us back—back to wholeness."

—LH, Founder and CEO,
Global Round Table Leadership

You already know that stories play a major role in both the Negotiation and Resignation phases. We've talked at length about the classic success story and how it's more fantasy than reality. We've talked about the stories we've inherited from our families and communities. We've talked about the systemic impact of thwarting and how our ambitions can often be manipulated to reflect someone else's wishes or how our pursuit can be hijacked by a distorted perception about what's required to succeed. So it shouldn't be surprising that as we enter the Renegotiation phase, stories will continue to play a central role. In fact, that's where we'll start. Only this time we'll focus on the stories we tell ourselves.

Every situation in which you've been supported or thwarted has left an imprint on you. And the way you carry those imprints either supports or thwarts your sense of your own value and what you believe is possible when it comes to your success. The stories you tell yourself about what happened, what it meant, and what you now believe as a result—this is how your past can dictate your present *and* future.

The dominant narratives in our lives are the baggage or inspiration we carry with us everywhere. So here is where we get to sift through them all, Marie Kondo–style, and ask ourselves: Does this story bring me joy? Does this story inspire me? Does this story serve a positive, forwarding role in my life? Or does it weigh me down, hold me back or, worse, create even more drama and trauma in my daily reality? And beneath all these questions: Where does this story even come from?

Many of us are living into inspiring stories that have been handed down over generations. This is an awesome thing because it gives us a sense of identity and purpose. But if the limiting stories go unchecked, they can stunt our growth and short circuit our happiness. Sometimes the stories we live into are created by people who love us or who are the keepers and protectors of our faith or lineage, and sometimes the stories we receive are created in the external world—and are *imposed* upon us by people who do not know or care about us and who may not be invested in our happiness nor our success.

To begin the process of Renegotiation, we need to ask ourselves— Whose story is it anyway? Understanding the origin of our stories can help us make sense of how and why those stories have shaped us for better or worse. It can also help us determine if it's a story we want to maintain or reclaim.

So what do I mean when I say reclaim?

Reclaiming is the process of taking back ownership of our own narrative and the right to define who you are and what you value. It's the process of deciding which stories you'll actively release or redefinition as you create new conditions for your life and your success.

Reclaiming is about re-establishing your own sense of identity and agency; in your life, work, and ultimately in how you show up in the world.

Reclaiming is a vital part of Renegotiation because it begins the process of internal *reconciliation*.

It's the place where we get to come home to ourselves—our thoughts, feelings, perspectives, and truth. It's the place where we finally make the decision to no longer be at war with ourselves.

In her groundbreaking book, the *5 Regrets of the Dying*, retired palliative care nurse Bronnie Ware shares that people's #1 regret is: "I wish I'd had the courage to live a life true to myself, not the life others expected of me."

This is what I believe is at the heart of our desire to Renegotiate. We want to trade in our threshold of tolerating somebody else's agenda for our own truth and the capacity to be alive, well and free.

How Do We Reclaim Our Stories *and* Our Lives?

There is a four-step process for reclaiming. It consists of re-membering, completing, liberating, and loving. These sacred (potent) practices are essential to Renegotiating because each practice unto itself has the potential to invite a new possibility. However, when these practices are combined, they have the ability to free us from all of the places we've been held back or down, by others, ourselves, and/or our society.

Sometimes we reclaim by simply changing the language of the story, sometimes by shifting our relationship to what happened and sometimes we reclaim by shifting our focus to *why* it happened in order to tell a completely different story. No matter what the approach, the intention is to put you in the driver's seat of your own journey.

Stage 1: Re-membering: What Happened?

In this first practice we listen very closely for the origin of the story—i.e. the initial incident, event, or experience. This stage is where we begin to separate what happened from the narrative that may be built around the incident. The story could originate from something we were told, or from something we experienced and/or witnessed first hand. In this step we separate what happened from the story about what happened. It's where we courageously tell the truth about what occurred and take responsibility for our participation in adopting this narrative (if appropriate). Finally, we examine how what happened (i.e. the incident, event, or experience) caused us to become estranged (disconnected) from our true selves. Here we also have the opportunity to acknowledge the impact this disconnect has had on our lives. We give ourselves permission to take courageous inventory. We give ourselves permission to grieve, and through the grieving process we *re-member* who we really are. As we *re-member*—we reclaim our power and agency. And we embrace our right to be whole again. This process ends with the mantra: *I AM Whole.*

Stage 2: Completion: What Wants to Be Released or Resolved?

In this second stage we confront all of the feelings. And we confront all of the thoughts and behaviors we may be clinging to as a result of what occurred and the story we've built around it. *What is it that we have believed that has given us this reality? Or this current state?* We actively chose to confront—then release—any part of this lingering story that does not empower us. We forgive and let go—this includes moving through any strong feelings we may possess towards ourselves and/or others. We embrace the lesson and corresponding wisdom of the experience. And we affirm to ourselves and others as needed that we are DONE. We take any actions that support our literal and symbolic resolution. This includes intimate and trusted sharing. This includes active reconciliation with ourselves and potentially with others. We reclaim our energy (from the past) and embrace our right to move on. This process ends with the mantra: *I AM or We Are Complete.*

Stage 3: Liberation: What Wants to Be Reimagined or Renegotiated?

This third stage acknowledges all of the space that opens up when we re-member who we are and let the past go. The wide open space we experience represents freedom and invites new possibilities for the creation of a new narrative. This is the place of inspiration and renewal. At this stage we feel the joy as we consider what we want to create in the void left by our old story. In this stage we open our hearts and minds to consider a whole new world of possibilities. We get to discover what feels more empowering and true given who we really are, what we value, and what we aspire to have and achieve. Now that we are whole and complete, we give ourselves permission to create something new. This process ends with the mantra: *I AM Free to Reimagine.*

Stage 4: Loving: What Wants to Be Newly Embraced or Embodied?

In this fourth and final stage, we return to ourselves and our natural state of love and compassion. We love and honor ourselves and we embrace our own magnificence. We appreciate this aspect of our journey and we recognize that we have made it to the other side. We are here in the present moment looking forward with a whole new perspective. We are older, wiser, more alive, and empowered. We reclaim our right to BE here now—in life; on the journey exactly as we are meant to be. We accept and celebrate that we are the architects of our own reality. This process ends with the mantra: *I AM True to Me.*

When we are immersed in a thwarted reality, it can take time to peel back all of the layers of our experience and unearth all of the narratives that may be operating. Some stories are readily available while others may be buried deep. The process of awakening and reclaiming is sacred ground and deserves to be met with the kind of patience and compassion we'd demonstrate toward our own child. Often it is our inner child who holds those remembrances.

Making the Journey from Wounded to True

This brings me to the story of a beloved client, Petuma, a successful thought leader and social media influencer.

> Petuma came to me because she was considering pivoting in a new direction. "Rha," she said, "I'm ready to shake things up!"
>
> "Awesome. Let's GO!" I replied. As we dug into her vision, I continued to marvel at her authenticity, humility, and grounded wisdom. There were aspects of her current business that she definitely loved, but there were other aspects and some team dynamics that were not working.
>
> We started talking about her threshold of tolerance, and I noticed there were several moments where she kept

disconnecting from the conversation. The deeper I went, the more silent she grew, only offering up a blank stare as she looked off into the distance. I had come to know this stare well. In my days of working with youth offenders, and in communities where the stories were riddled with one traumatic narrative after the next, I learned that sometimes it was just easier to check out when conversations landed a little too close to home. "Hey, where did you go?" I asked. She sighed, then nodded, almost as if making a clear internal choice, she turned back to me, her eyes filled with tears.

"I've been thinking about toleration and why I've let the situation with a member of my team get so bad. I just realized I have a history of tolerating this kind of abuse not in my business per se but definitely in other areas." Petuma went on to share a devastating story of how she was terrorized in a long-term love relationship and all she endured before she was finally able to break free.

"This feels like that, all over again," she reflected.

When we dug deeper, we unearthed the narrative that made it possible for this team member to treat her so poorly and still be on her team: "If someone is unhappy, it's your job to fix it." She blamed herself for this person's failure to succeed on the team. The worse they performed, the more they pointed the finger, and every time they pointed the finger this narrative would play and she would feel responsible. And because she felt responsible, she continued to jump through hoops to try to make it better. What she did not realize until we began to talk about it was that this person's behavior reminded her of her ex- boyfriend, and before him, her mother's ex-boyfriend. And unbeknownst to her, she was using this scenario to try to fix what happened in each of those scenarios too. As we got to the heart of what was happening, I asked her to speak her truth.

"This person is not taking responsibility for their lack of results, and I've basically indulged their BS." She said, "Wow!" then began laughing as the realization hit her. "I'm trying to make them be something they are not and they resent me for it. Oh, God." We both sat in silence, allowing the power of this realization to take hold. "Okay, well, this is gonna stop today." She said definitively.

Ever so gently and slowly over the next five sessions we began to unpack the bigger story. By the time we got to stage 2, she was working through the emotions of dealing with this challenging team member and the painful history with her ex-boyfriend. (She wasn't ready to tackle her mom's situation yet.) Needless to say, there was a lot of forgiving and releasing happening: forgiving the actions of the team member, forgiving certain decisions and forgiving herself. We cycled back to this stage several times, especially as she began to take the actions associated with removing this person from her team. My job was to hold the space for one narrative at a time while keeping track of when other narratives emerged and gently guiding her back to the central dominating one.

When we arrived at stage 3, the new narrative she gave voice to went something like this:

"I deserve to be honored, respected and well supported. I'm building a world-class team that holds a deep reverence for the vision and for each other. If someone is unhappy, we each do our part and take full responsibility for our respective and collective results."

Petuma worked with this new narrative, repeating it over and over to herself—posting it in her office space and placing it as a screensaver on her phone. She even created an alarm that reminded her to repeat the mantra throughout the day. By the time she got to stage 4, we were celebrating. The team member had been transitioned, and she was on the hunt for their replacement with a kind of laser clarity and precision about what she wanted beyond just the right knowledge and skill sets. As she turned to her love life, she used this new narrative to create a whole new standard for the kind of partnership she was looking for.

She felt a new level of self love and appreciation emerge through this process because she was willing to reclaim her safety and her dignity. "I feel so strong and clear right now," she said. "I know what I want and I know what I need."

The process of reclamation is an ancient practice—many cultures and traditions have anointed designated members in their community who are the keepers of the stories of their existence. Because it is through the stories that we tell that we come to understand who we are, where we've been, and where we're going.

In our modern society, we've lost this; so many of us struggle to find that sense of belonging and connection—and dare I say, a sense of identity—because we've allowed contributions to our story that may not actually honor the truth of who we really are.

So from today forward, *you* are the keeper of your story. Your life is a living, breathing narrative, one that you are co-creating in real time with the visions, hopes, and dreams you carry—and the beliefs, thoughts, and behaviors you choose. Through your thoughts, your feelings, your actions, your speech, you are creating *yourself*, and the more awareness and intention you bring to that creation, the better off you'll be. Our stories represent our lives—not just the past but the present and future. Reclaiming them increases our potential to live a life that's more authentic and aligned. And alignment—a necessary step on the road to fulfillment—is where we'll turn next.

Your Terms

1. Take a moment to identify one story that you'd like to reclaim as it relates to your new or evolving definition of success.

2. Use the four-step reclamation protocol to release the old narrative and embrace a new more empowering story.

3. Create a two- or three-sentence version of the story that enables you to give voice to the reality you now want to create for yourself as you begin to Renegotiate. Use Petuma's example to inspire you.

For more downloadable tools and resources, go to: www.move thecrowd.me/IA-resources.

Chapter 8

Realigning: The Truth about Getting True

"We are reckoning with a greater level of truth. The truth will set you free—there's a lot of freedom in truth. But it requires us to let go of the past and look deeply at what matters."

—CH, Corporate Change Agent

As much as I profess that I'm not a doctor, you must know, I'm *really* not a mechanic! But there is one part of vehicle maintenance that's central to Renegotiating, and that's alignment. When a car's wheels are out of alignment, the whole driving experience is affected, from steering and handling (you're trying to go one way; your wheels have a different idea) to fuel economy (the extra effort to make your car go where you want it to gobbles up gas) to safety (misaligned tires wear out unevenly, which can damage the tires and wheels and potentially lead to dangerous blow-outs).

When something is out of alignment, it's also called being out of true. Boy, do I love that phrase! When your work or your working style is out of alignment, it means it doesn't sync up with *your* truth—your true self, your true values, what's truly best for you. Even when you "succeed," if your misalignment is sustained, your energy is chronically drained, and you can suffer actual, sometimes serious, physical and psychological harm.

Just think of all the conversations we've had about trauma, burn-out, and fatigue in the past few years and even in this book. That's because any time we're pushing, grinding, or forcing, we're out of alignment. Anytime we're diminishing, minimizing, or avoiding, we're out of alignment. Anytime we're disrupting, suppressing, manipulating, or blocking the natural order and flow—yep, out of alignment. And as with a car, all this thwarted energy equates to a loss of power. And believe me, powerlessness is expensive!

So, just like we need to reclaim, we need to realign.

This is the part of Renegotiating that calls for the greatest courage, because it usually requires facing some hard truths.

It also requires stepping back. Because just as a car's wheels can't be realigned while the car is on the road, you can't realign while going about business as usual. This is *very* challenging for many of my clients. After all, in our culture, business as usual so often means *busy-ness* as usual. We are devoted to being busy. Being busy means you're important. And for many of us, just like our job titles or roles, it has become an integral part of our identity.

In a perfect world, we could all take the occasional sabbatical to give ourselves time away to refuel and reconnect. I'm not talking about a vacation (which usually involves other people and their agendas). I'm talking about real time spent with just you and you. Time to actually slow down. Time to take stock, and *listen* to your higher wisdom, and gain perspective. I call this sacred or powerful pausing. In the real world, it is almost never an option. But if you are genuinely committed to improving the quality of your life and working in ways that are far more authentic and meaningful, then you *must* set aside quality time to build a more authentic and meaningful relationship with yourself. Take your pick: vacation days, Sundays, Tuesday nights, every morning from 5:00 to 6:00—whenever you can commit to doing the sacred work of realigning.

Realigning involves come-to-Jesus reflections about the concessions you've made (remember that list I invited you to make in Chapter 2?) and reckoning with the distance between where they've led you and where you really want to be.

Realigning involves coming face-to-face with your values and what is really important to you and revisiting the promises you've made to yourself but may not be living up to.

Realigning involves taking an inventory of where you're selling yourself—or your soul —short. Where you're tolerating less than you deserve. Where you're acting in ways that are outside your own true nature and causing harm in the process.

When you realign, you consult your values and the things you value. And you consider your resources, in the form of your time, your talent, your finances and your energy.

Taking all these things into account, you ask yourself questions like: How do I feel about my work right now? What is getting most of my time and energy? Where do I feel vibrant and strong? Where do I feel totally frustrated or drained? Do I feel appreciated in my current role? Am I getting the support I need? Have I told X, Y, and Z how I really feel?

Depending upon how far off course you've gone, the call to realign can feel *scary*. If you've held your tongue or sat down on your truths for a very long time, it can feel to some as if you're coming out of left field. Or if you get quiet you may realize that e-v-e-r-y-thing has to change. When you confront all of the "outages" it can make you want to press the snooze button for those precious 10 more minutes of sleep.

You can tell yourself whatever you like. However, your energy does not lie, and it will only be a matter of time before you're forced to confront those disconnects. Sadly, for many of us those moments come at the expense of our health and well-being. We run out of gas, or as in the analogy above—we blow a tire—and are forced off the road.

Speed is one of the greatest challenges to alignment. When we don't want to deal with our own disappointment and pain, we can easily find something else to do. But with speed also comes mistakes, missed cues, and even neglect. Speed can even produce a lack of compassion and an impatience with ourselves and others that over time can stack up as wreckage.

The good news is if we can get off of the hamster wheel (or out of the rat race)—we may be surprised to find a new level of clarity and strength as we go to answer these important questions. With reclaiming, we take back our stories. With realignment, we take back our energy! And with the restoring of our energy comes our real power.

The Six Frontiers of Renegotiation

When we seek to realign, it's important that we take a comprehensive look at what's happening in every aspect of our lives. As much as many of us want to believe that we operate in silos and that we're awesome at compartmentalizing, we may find that it just ain't so. There are six important frontiers that are worthy to examine when we consider Realigning: health and well-being, financial viability and sustainability, purpose and fulfillment, relationships and community, conducive environment, and quality of your day-to-day.

Health and Well-Being

What used to be the final frontier for so many of us is now becoming the *foundation* of anything we want to do, be, or have in our lives. Our mental, physical, spiritual, and emotional health is everything. Without it, all else is compromised. When we consider each aspect, we may find that we've been giving lots of attention to some areas while totally neglecting the importance of others. For example, our physical well-being, from a cosmetic perspective, may have ranked high on the list. However, having an attractive body and killer hair is not necessarily the same as really caring for our physical anatomies. We also know that pre-pandemic, we didn't have a lot of room to even talk openly about our mental health; more less actively tend to it. So as we begin to consider this first frontier, we may find that there's real work to do.

First, let's get grounded in how you define your well-being: Do you have a vision for each of these areas? Are you able to tell when something is off? Are there chronic areas of discomfort or distress that need to be addressed? Are there rituals and habits that you've wanted to start but have not been able to get to? Are there places where you know you need support? Use these prompts to just begin exploring.

Financial Viability and Sustainability

This frontier is often considered the **main** frontier, and we can either hyper-focus or under-focus to the detriment of everything else. As you examine the state of your financial reality, what do you see? As you consider your relationship with work and money, is there a positive connection? Considering what you earn (or acquire) and the way you earn (or acquire), what feels important to acknowledge for yourself?

Many of us have been reexamining our value and the degree to which we believe our earnings are indeed in alignment with our contributions. In a world where it seems that so many are struggling, especially when it comes to money, it's important to consider how your new or evolving definition of success is reflected in your finances. For some of you, under-earning may be a real issue that must be addressed. For others, earning may not be the issue for you but rather *how* your strategy for earning may be compromising the other vital areas of your life (health, relationships, etc.) For others still, you may find that what's happening in the other areas of your life are in some way compromising your financial viability.

Whatever the case may be, here's your opportunity to explore. What is your vision for financial success? How does that align with your current reality? Is there a particular amount that feels more aligned with your current contribution than what you're actually receiving right now? When it comes to your finances, what have your toughest challenges been? Get as specific as you can here. Are you needing to create more opportunities to save or invest? Are you needing to put yourself first financially in ways you never have before? Are you being called to manage your resources differently—what do you see?

Purpose and Fulfillment

This is yet another hot spot especially as we consider the previous chapters where we've explored our own Resignation. For some of you, you may realize that a pivot to a new field is what you desire, for others you may love the work you do—but just aspire to design your workday differently; for others, you may not have found your true north yet but you see an opportunity in your current role to learn and grow in ways that make this the right opportunity *for now.* Get clear about where purpose and fulfillment are either present or lacking for you.

Ask yourself: What is my vision for how purpose and meaning show up in my work? Am I passionate about my current work? Am I doing work that I'm proud of? Is my work structured in a way that's fulfilling? Am I inspired by the ultimate aim and mission? Am I inspired by the people around me? Am I working in ways that make the lives and realities of others better? What else feels important to consider when you think about work that is meaningful to you?

Realigning around purpose can sometimes feel like a luxury. But at the risk of perpetuating someone else's ambitions, and postponing your own happiness, you've gotta go here even if you start with a little "p" and work your way up to your life's work.

Relationships and Community

Some of us were incredibly lucky to have our most cherished relationships deepen during the pandemic. Locked away in our cool pods, we hung with our folks and also created phenomenal co-parenting and working scenarios that built lasting bonds even to this day. For others of us, we may have felt like we were being sentenced because we could no longer use our endeavors outside of the house to escape. No matter what the case, It's important to acknowledge that we are different—and that may mean that our prerequisites for relationship and community have changed.

As you consider your most intimate relationships, do they feel aligned with where you are now? Do they still meet your hopes, needs, and desires? Are you finding yourself drawn to the same people you were even one to two years ago, or has something shifted? Is there any place where you want or need to make amends? When you consider what you've traditionally looked to your community to provide do you find that they are indeed providing it? For those of you who may have been struggling with a lack of community pre-pandemic, have you found that it's gotten better or worse? What do you need to thrive in a relationship? Look at the personal *and* professional. What do you need to thrive in a network or community? Consider this question from the perspective of what you'd like to bring and what you'd like to receive.

As you clarify your criteria for support and human connection you'll have a better sense of what is aligning and not aligning for you. It may take real courage to tell the truth here—but I want you to do it.

Conducive Environment

This frontier is vital but often underestimated. Who and what you surround yourself with can be the difference between creating your best work ever or wasting precious resources and time. One of the biggest pushbacks as we emerged from the pandemic has been going back into the office. Why? Because so many people found their secret formula to greater productivity working from home. The time they got back from the multi-hour bumper-to-bumper commute, the ability to shut the door or exit out of the video conference and really not be disturbed. The ability to get in a nature walk with the dog in the middle of the day to help fuel our inspiration well into the evening hours.

When we could finally control our environment and our work process and flow—all kinds of great things happened. For others of us we couldn't wait to return to our co-working spaces or offices fast enough. We hungered for the social connection, for the camaraderie of working hands on with our teams; we even craved the boundaries of having our work in one designated place while our living space was in another. Sometimes it wasn't even about the people but more about the space itself.

As you consider your current environment, do you find it to be conducive to the work you want or need to do? Do you have a vision for your ideal space? What aspects of design and location feel really important to you? If your work environment doesn't feel aligned for you—what do you notice is missing? As you consider Renegotiating, how important is this frontier for you?

Quality of Your Day-to-Day

This last frontier often sneaks up on people. As I shared in my own meltdown in Chapters 2 and 5, one of my biggest takeaways was that the way I was working *was* the greatest source of my misery. In the traditional success formula, it's been all about the results with no regard for how you get there nor for the subsequent toll it may take on any other aspect of your life.

Now that we're Renegotiating, we have an opportunity to consider; what is the nature of my current work experience? And what do I want my experience of work to be? Loving what you do is just a part of the equation. Having greater joy, fun, ease, and flow *in the experience* is something we are all starting to consider. As our tolerance thresholds have adjusted, many people admit that there have been dramatic shifts in their expectations for where they'll work, how long they'll work, and in what way they desire to meet the demands of their respective roles. What is the quality of your day-to-day like? What aspects of your working day feel the most joyful for you? Which aspects feel most challenging?

Many of us are still healing toxic work experiences—so to even consider that our work process can be joyful and enriching is new. This cannot be swept aside. Getting to our own clarity about what matters to us in the day-to-day is vital for Realigning.

Having the Courage to Stop

Putting on the brakes is never easy. Anytime I make this recommendation to my clients, they always blow right past it. Though I believe the notion of extended time off is gaining greater popularity, for many it continues to be a wish that they are conveniently avoiding.

- "I don't know what I'd do with myself."
- "I'm someone who needs to be moving—if I'm not busy, I'm not in a good place."
- "I've got way too much to do to even consider it—my kids, what will happen with them?"
- "Some of us don't have the privilege of taking a break and it feels insensitive to even imply that some people can afford to do this given all of the inequality we face."
- "Who's going to pay my bills? If I don't hustle I don't eat."
- "I can't totally unplug—there's no way I could go off the grid—something would break, I'm sure of it."

This is just a small sampling of what I hear. But I've witnessed and held people from all backgrounds and all socioeconomic levels through a realignment process that has enabled them to emerge stronger, brighter, clearer, more capable, and empowered on the other side.

The process of realignment is not always a function of time, it's more a function of discipline. Hearing the call to pause, following your instincts, clearing out all the distractions, sitting with your own thoughts and feelings, confronting your fears, regrets, anxieties, and aspirations. This is the work. The time involved has everything to do with how long it takes a person to *really get quiet*. Then it's a matter of how open and willing they are to confront the state of their lives and tell the truth about what they see. Then it's about giving yourself what you need to heal and restore. Finally, it's about the degree to which they are ready to have something else other than the status quo.

> My beloved client Dynia, an empowerment coach, totally took the bull by the horns and gave herself almost a whole year off. "When the pandemic hit full force, I went into mama bear mode. So many of my people were going through it, and I wanted to be there for them. I was holding space in our coaching sessions, in community support circles, on social media—it was A-LOT!" In addition to her clients, Dynia was watching her aging parents out of the corner of her eye. She was holding down her beloved partner, and helping him watch his aging parents too. "As if that wasn't enough, I wound up launching a new program right in the middle of George Floyd. I was using a model that was 'proven' sure, but not necessarily right for me." She paused.
>
> "Finally, I just reached my own breaking point and I had to go dark. At the time I had no idea how long, but I knew it had to be at least a few months. Before I did it, I had to think it through: How would I tell my partner? How would

I cover bills? What would I say to my clients? There was so much back and forth going on in my head. So much fear about what would happen if I just stopped. But once I finally made the decision and told myself, 'I'm doing this!' all of these incredible things started to happen. My partner got a very lucrative project, my aunt mailed me a dividend check from a payout on some investment she put my name on, I got a low-interest loan, and all of a sudden this decision got really real." For the first couple of months, Dynia just rested. "I had no idea how exhausted I really was." The next couple of months she began to listen: "I was having this chronic pain in my body and I knew it was about more than just normal fatigue. My body was trying to tell me something. And the more I ignored it, the louder the pain got." As Dynia found the courage to listen, she discovered that there was a huge part of her creative expression that she'd been burying. With that realization came a whole host of narratives about worthiness and practicality. Fueled by this realization, Dynia began to explore what caused her to abandon that part of herself.

"When I did the Six Frontiers exercise there were all kinds of skeletons that came tumbling out of the closet. I was forced to confront all of the places where I put myself last. I knew that I was being called to something greater, but I had a lot of fear, and that fear kept me in hiding, helping everyone else be amazing and bring *their* thing to life."

There were times during her sabbatical where Dynia got worked up around money. "Even though I had simplified my life and was doing pretty good between my partner and my savings, I was still worried. But the moment I tried to throw myself back into action, I'd feel totally drained of energy. I knew that I couldn't run from these realizations. I just had to put on my big girl pants and deal with them." One by one Dynia began to take on these old stories; she reclaimed them and created new conversations.

"As I emerged from this work I could feel my energy growing and feel my creativity coming back. I was getting all kinds of ideas about what could be next." One of Dynia's greatest desires was to start a podcast, so she did. As Dynia began to work on her podcast and design her new offerings she got really excited. "I was buzzing with energy and joy and I couldn't wait to dive in and go to work." She said that the real test, however, was when the opportunities and invitations started rolling in once she returned. "With every new request I sat with it, then felt into my heart, is it a yes or a no? And I honored whatever my energy told me."

When I asked Dynia what her greatest learnings were from this process she replied, "My clarity and my vibrancy are too important to squander. I've decided that from now on I'm only going to do what feels good to me."

The realigning process is never a one and done, but your initial reset gives you a strong foundation for how to build in the practice of powerful pausing and checking in. Sometimes it only takes a minute to recognize when something is off and only another two to three minutes to course correct. Sometimes, it may take you a bit longer. The gift of this process is that it invites a new level of awareness and attunement that gives you another source of power as you begin to Renegotiate on behalf of *your* wants, needs, and desires.

Your Terms

1. Take a moment to step back—even if it's just for a weekend. Challenge yourself to stop for three days: no devices, no media, no being "on call." Create your own personal getaway and spend some quality time with you and you.

2. During that quality time, use the Six Frontiers to take a personal inventory of where you may be feeling called to realign. As you move through each area, notice the thoughts and feelings associated with each realigning opportunity.

3. Keep track of the conversations that you may need to have with yourself and others—to support getting back on track i.e. in alignment with your time, values, resources, and energy.

For more downloadable tools and resources, go to: www.move thecrowd.me/IA-resources.

Reimagining: A More Successful Definition of Success

"It was a part of my world view, that whatever work might mean, that it could be meaningful, it could be of service, it could be a part of my vocational calling."
—RB, Founding Partner BBMG

It's not enough to abandon the traditional story of success. I know that whole movements have been built on the backs of the "anti" this or that, but I promise you, anything that defines itself in reaction to something it does *not* want only perpetuates a relationship with more of the same. If we aren't clear by this point about anything else when it comes to our work and the way we work, it's that more of the same just isn't gonna cut it.

This brings me to the third and final aspect of the Renegotiation process, which is the place of Reimagination. Remember when we were kids? If we were fortunate enough to be surrounded by love, and a strong, foundational home, we'd hear the phrase "go out and play." But of course, as we get older, play becomes less and less of a mandate and the phrase "go out and work" naturally takes its place.

A vital part of our well-being lives in our ability to dream and imagine. When our innate sense of creativity is at the center of our work—we thrive!

Our happiness matters. Our sense of freedom and autonomy matter. So does our sense of creativity and fulfillment.

Reimagining is the bridge we built between "I'm out" and "I'm all in." It's where we move from being disillusioned to being deeply invested.

Reimagining is the place where we invite ourselves to expand the lens on what's possible. Where we go beyond what is ingrained and familiar to discover what is better than we ever could have envisioned.

Reimagining is where we actively and intentionally shape a new reality for our lives and our work. Where our values are recognized, where our greater purpose takes form and where our contributions matter.

> This takes me to the story of GANGGANG. GANGGANG is an Indianapolis-based creative agency with one goal: to amplify the work of creatives of color. In 2021 they were all set to curate an exhibit at the Indianapolis Museum of Art—a big deal for a fledgling organization—when something crazy happened. The museum posted a job opening that said it was looking for a director who, among other things, would maintain "the Museum's traditional, core, white art audience." You read that right, and yes, this was 2021.
>
> What happened next was a case study in the Negotiation/ Resignation/Renegotiation continuum. Initially, GANG-GANG's founders responded by trying to negotiate (aka navigate) the current situation. They gave the museum a list of conditions under which they'd move forward with the exhibit. But the museum wouldn't play ball. So GANGGANG resigned—as in Resignation 2.0 ("peace out!"): Though

they were only a few months old, they walked away from a showcase opportunity at one of the largest museums in the country. And then they began renegotiating: reassessing their ambitions, reclaiming their agency and their story, realigning with their values, and reimagining the terms of their success.

To repeat: They reimagined the terms of their success.

Four years later, GANGGANG is now best known as the force behind Butter, a fine-art fair re-envisioned: not in New York or London or Paris or Miami Beach, but in Indianapolis; not including a smattering of Black artists, but comprising only Black artists; not settling for the old financial model, but giving 100 percent of the proceeds from sold art back to the artists. When you consult their website, you're met by this bold mission statement:

"GANGGANG activates the creative economy to center beauty, equity and culture in cities. We believe that culture brings humanity together and that art challenges mindsets. It is our vision to build new ecosystems that center the care and economic viability of creatives. We do that via programming, advocacy and production."

It is a glowing example of what it means to actively reimagine an industry and world that works to support the economic viability and sustainability of creatives. They've expanded their exhibits beyond Butter and are now touring in various cities throughout the United States with a commitment to supporting local artists in those cities along the way.[1,2]

Would you call this success? I sure would. It's a fantastic example of how it really is possible to conceive of new ways of working based on your values and your vision for what your life and your work should look like. GANGGANG was able to walk away from their curating gig at the museum because, as good as it would have looked on their resumé, it would have violated their commitment to true equity and inclusion. They knew who they were and what they stood for. They were aligned and ready to Reimagine.

Reimagining is the place where you get to be your own hero and tell a success story that authentically aligns with who you are and what you believe. It's the place where you get to dream. To draw on inspiration to fuel your highest purpose and lay the ground for meaningful contribution.

Gathering the Strength to Dream

Whether you connect to a spiritual path, follow a religious doctrine, or simply believe in the concepts of creativity and love, inspiration is vital to our ability to dream and Reimagine. We are aspirational by nature, and when those aspects of our expression are stifled, we are operating at a fraction of our true capacity. Think about all of the years you may have worked consumed by stress and fear. Now imagine what it would be like to be fueled by something greater.

The science and the data support that when we're able to access elevated states of being and experience a sense of wonder and awe, we tap into other dimensions of our wisdom, creativity, brilliance, and innovation.

According to the Flow Research Collective, a "flow state" is an optimal state of awareness that enables performance to go through the roof. Thirty years of neuroscience research has found that flow state is responsible for all the skills we most need in the twenty-first-century workplace. Increasing productivity by 500 percent, creativity by 600 percent, and skill acquisition by 230 percent.[3]

It can arrive in the midst of a playful improvisational riff or in the immersive state of concentration that encourages time to stand still. No matter what we call it—"catching the spirit" or "being in the zone"— our hearts and souls hunger for this place. This is where our greatest ideas and innovations live. This is where our most euphoric work takes place. This is where our souls come alive and our truth comes rushing in.

When we are in the realm of (Re)imagination, the quality of our working experience *feels* different. Our level of joy, satisfaction, and fulfillment is high even when we are putting forth effort on a massive scale. Tapping into our muse gives us the permission to play, to experiment, and to explore new frontiers and horizons. And when we do, we actually arrive—present—in our full potential and power. Reclamation brings us back into the heart. Realignment brings us back into the body. Reimagination brings us back into our spirits. Back into the source of our greatest aspiration—to be our most authentic self in service to our highest contribution.

A vital part of our Renegotiation includes reserving the right to be inspired—about our lives and about our work. Inspiration is a 360-degree proposition.

This means you get to explore the possibility of being the person you've always wanted to be; of doing the work that you really love; of operating in ways that are joyful, enriching, and uplifting.

This is where you begin to redefine *your* story of success—on *your* terms. With a blank canvas and an open slate you get to be challenged and affirmed as you reach for the next level of your own growth and evolution.

When we set the stage of Reimagining, this is the energy we want to call in. We want to feel this sense of optimism—we want to open up to this more expansive, receptive, and creative space inside of ourselves so that our higher knowledge, wisdom, and awareness can drop in.

As you consider your vision for success and the kind of relationship you want to have with your work, what do you see? Even before we get into the specificity of what that work is, it's important that we put our work in its proper perspective.

As we draw on the insights and choices made through the work of Reclaiming our stories and Realigning with our values, in this final stage of the Renegotiation process, it's time to become very intentional about what we seek to create.

Answering the Call

When we explored those six frontiers in Chapter 8, I called out that a central part of our Renegotiation would be around purpose and meaning. Who are you? And what are you here for? Some of you may have never asked yourself these questions prior to the pandemic, yet here we are. And I *am* asking. Your answers will be vital to our Reimagination process.

In the many conversations I've had doing this work and in writing this book, I've found that people who've connected to a greater sense of purpose coming out of the pandemic are happier, more empowered, and ready to thrive in comparison to those who've yet to strongly consider it. Like I said at the top, if all of this is just about the next company or the next promotion, or the next client—you may be missing the point. Go bigger, dig deeper, and ask yourself, "What do I *really* want?" You don't have to have all of the answers at this moment, and I promise in the chapters ahead I will get to your potential concerns. But for now—even if it's just for the duration of this chapter—I want to encourage you to take the constraints off and really listen. Sit in a quiet place, bring your attention to your breath, and re-ask the question, "What do I really want?" Have your journal ready so that you can capture whatever comes through.

For those of you who may already know what your work is, this next section might be about challenging yourself to consider your *way* of working.

The call can take shape and form in so many ways, what's most important is to understand that it's here to guide you through this next chapter of life and work in a way that invites more of what you want, need, and desire in a way that feels more empowering to you.

Use this moment to open your mind, your ears, your eyes, and your heart. Feel those impulses and urges as they move through you. Take this new level of clarity and energy with you as you dive into the next section.

Five Ws and an H!

The process of Reimagining is fueled by creating a visceral experience that defines what you want to have, do, and be. The specificity we bring to redefining our success and each aspect of our work is what begins to make it real—in our minds, in our hearts, and ultimately in our world. See this section as a stream of consciousness exercise, imagine yourself in a quiet space, in a setting where you feel comfortable just focusing on you. I recommend having a journal and something to write with handy for the questions ahead.

What

Let's start by getting crystal clear about *what it is* that you want your work to do. GANGGANG wanted to amplify the work of creatives of color. What is your intention for your work? What is the ultimate contribution you want to make? Further, what are the unique gifts and talents that you wish to share? What kinds of opportunities would really excite you and enable you to bring what you want to bring? (Yep, money can and should be factored in here!) When you think about the kind of work that would give you the greatest amount of joy and fulfillment, what do you see?

Who

Next, let's talk about *who you most want to serve* and who you'd love to collaborate with. You can let your wish list run wild here. More important than specific names are the qualities and characteristics—the values, skills, and temperaments—of the people you want to spend time with. Who do you want to make the greatest difference for, and why?

This is an important moment, because in my experience *everyone* wants to make a difference; it's how we know our lives matter. And everyone wants to collaborate with people who see them, people they feel they can learn from as well as trust, honor, and respect. So who are *your* people? When you think about the difference you want to make, it's important to have a connection to who you are making that difference for just as when you think about your fellow contributors you want to feel a connection to the people you get to do this important work with.

Where

Now let's dive into the question of *where*. Think about the Realigning work we did around the need for a Conducive Environment in Chapter 8. This could be about literal location, but it's more about the type of environments that motivate and inspire you and would really enable you to thrive. Are you someone who needs nature or quiet? Or does your creativity depend on the buzzing hustle-and-bustle energy and lots of give-and-take? Do you need the structure of going to an office? Do you do your best work reclining in bed? What do you notice when you ask yourself these questions? Space is such a crucial factor when it comes to what enables us to do work that we love and enjoy. I also want you to consider how that space needs to be set up to best support you—what elements of design and flow feel important to give voice to here as well?

How

Next, we'll look at *how* you want to work. What rhythms, structures, strategies and practices really let you bring your best? Do you like collaborating or calling the shots? Working in a corporate structure or entrepreneurially? Devoting yourself to one all-consuming project at a time or having many fingers in many pies all at once? 9-to-5 or more free-range? Beneath all of this, how do you want to *feel* when you work, and how do you want to feel *about* your work? What is the quality of experience you want to have in your day-to-day? Everyone has their own style—the goal is to get real about yours.

We've all had experiences working in more traditional hierarchies, but I think the work of the future is leaning towards more collaborative and dynamic models. In addition, more episodic project-based opportunities that have real space and rest built into the structure are also becoming more desirable for many: autonomy with connection, inspiration with guidance and direction as needed, opportunities to lead with an eye toward how to motivate and inspire others with dignity. Give yourself the freedom to really get outside of the box here.

Why

This is the heart of the matter. When it comes to having a more meaningful existence in life and in work you want to be clear about *why*. *Why is this work important to you?* Why are these people important to you? Why is this location, environment, background important? Why is *the way you* do this work important? What aspects of your most authentic self get to be expressed through this work? In what ways do your talents, gifts, and abilities thrive? Who do you become when you do this work? In what ways does this work make you, your life, and our world better? Where does your greatest satisfaction lie? We're here for greater joy, freedom, and fulfillment, remember? So think about why.

When

Finally, we'll think about *when:* the timeline for when you'll start working towards this vision. Some people get to this point and are 100 percent ready to take the plunge and make a change. Other people need a transition plan; they're not ready to dive right into uncertain waters without a clear direction for where and how to swim.

Like GANGGANG, you may have to move swiftly in response to a crisis, or you may have a longer runway. Whatever your situation, think about timing in a way that acknowledges reality but discourages fear-based stalling. Because in the end, reimagining isn't about shaking things up for the sake of shaking them up. It's about seeing *viable* alternatives to the status quo. It's about inviting new possibilities that will make your life so much better.

As the realizations in each of the areas unfold and you discover the distance between where you are now and where you aspire to be it can feel challenging to put a timeline on it. Especially if you feel that you've got a ton of considerations to address along the way. Do not worry about that right now; just take a moment to recognize that you've got the beginnings of a blueprint—one we'll continue to flesh out—in the chapters to come.

GANGGANG took the leap with a clarity and conviction that has absolutely paid off. You can too. Once you've imagined those alternatives and possibilities, you may find it hard to go back. That means it's finally time to start making them happen—which is what the final parts of the book, i.e., the how-to parts, are all about.

Your Terms

1. Revisit the question in "Gathering the Strength to Dream": "What do you really want?"

2. Revisit the question in "Answering The Call": "What is your vision and new definition for Success?"

3. Set aside about 90 minutes and do the Reimagination process (5Ws and an H). Give yourself the freedom to respond to the prompts in a way that truly unearths what you'd like this next chapter of life and work to be about.

For more downloadable tools and resources, go to: www.move thecrowd.me/IA-resources.

Reimagining: A More Successful Definition of Success

Part IV

How to Renegotiate with Yourself

No single part of this book is more important than any other, but in my 30 years of experience working with clients, Parts IV through VI are full of the stuff people *really* want to know—the "how-to" stuff.

So let's get to it!

In the Resignation phase, many of us think there's no possibility of change—work is work, the system is the system, and our two choices are to suck it up or leave. But when we're in a bad work situation, and even if we've recently left one, it can be as though we're suffering from clinical depression or even PTSD—our perception of reality is often skewed. And that skewed perception can linger. Even as we start doing the work of Renegotiation—reclaiming our stories, realigning with our values, reimagining success—many of us are still listening to an inner voice telling us *It is what it is. Change? Yeah right. Good luck with that.*

I'm here to tell you: that inner voice is wrong. The truth is, just as our culture's definition of success is a *created story*, our system of work is a *created system*. It's manmade (and yes, I do mean "man"). And that's good news—great news!—because what was made can be unmade—and remade better. Recent history is full of dramatic examples of revolutionary reversals that once seemed impossible, from the fall of the Berlin Wall to the end of Apartheid to the legalization of gay marriage. We have just as strong a legacy of rising up to achieve what seemed impossible as we do of grinning and bearing it.

But there's no hope of changing the workplace—or the world—until we are willing to change ourselves. And so our internal Renegotiation begins—with an invitation to examine our mindset about change, to discover a new level of permission, and to make peace with our true and intentional ambitions.

Changing Your Mindset about Change

"The business is about shifting consciousness; it's about how to soften the resistance to transformation."

—MS, Actor, Director, Educator

In my work I routinely encounter deep skepticism about the possibility of systemic change, especially in my work with underrepresented communities—i.e., women, people of color, people from the LGBTQ+ community, etc. There's often a sense that the only way such change could even hope to occur is with the total dismantling of all existing structures, guided by a leader who, like Dr. Martin Luther King Jr. or Gandhi, is almost superhuman in their vision, their abilities, their charisma, and their willingness to risk and sacrifice everything in order to upend the status quo.

We discount the possibility of change as we count ourselves out as change-makers—even more so if we come from a culture with deeply ingrained conditioning about risk aversion. If we have traumatic and violent examples of the repercussions of making change, then change is absolutely off the table.

But remember what we said in Chapter 9: reimagining happens when you get to tell a success story that authentically aligns with who you are and what you believe. To make change happen, you don't have to be a hero to the world. You can start by being a hero to yourself—by keeping the promises you've made to yourself about being real and doing more of what really matters.

There's a generational piece at work here, too. Call it cynicism or "realism" or the scars of Jim Crow, Vietnam, and Watergate, but mainstream Baby Boomers and a sizeable percentage of Gen Xers tend to pooh-pooh the possibility of changing the system in a way that Millennials and members of Gen Z don't—and, let's be real, can't.

The younger generations represent the evolution of our optimism *and* our threshold of tolerance. Collectively, their tolerance is lower; they don't hesitate to call out dysfunction and call for new and better. If you're part of the system they're calling out, that can be uncomfortable! (and yes, sometimes problematic too—I promise, I'll get there in a later chapter). But if you can put aside the discomfort, for now, there's something to be learned. Millennials have proved themselves masters of making change from the outside (think of the disrupters behind the share and tech economies, who've built companies like Airbnb, Google, Uber, etc.). And Gen Z, the generation that has given new life to labor unions, is showing up to make change from within. Of course, they face challenges as they Negotiate (as in Navigate) old structures, but their reverence for new ideas and their willingness to put their efforts where their convictions lie is worthy of note.

If you're someone who believes "It is what it is," then I want you to look critically at that belief, where it comes from, and how it may be keeping you stuck in an unwanted place. Though we've logically said goodbye to our Resignation, it can be easy to slip back into the status quo, like a comfy old pair of sneakers.

Standing still, our reimagined world sounds amazing, but when we go to move, something happens—as we bump up against the confines of our reality, we get scared, and our immediate instinct is to pull away—to run back to safety. In our conditioned response, we go right back to hiding out, or playing safe and/or playing small. And we abandon our commitment to doing the work that would enable us to move beyond our doubts and fears to chart a new path through the unknown.

The capacity we want to build here is the kind that will enable you to put your aspirations on the court in service to the change you want to be and see—one step at a time. So we begin by asking, "What would you need to *believe* in order to know that change is possible—for you? "Where are you willing to challenge yourself in the name of moving closer to *your* desired vision?"

This brings me to the story of Freda, a dynamic communications consultant who joined an amazing nonprofit that was founded and led by the wife of a prominent businessman.

> Early on in the position, Freda began to notice that as much as she (i.e. the wife as Executive Director) was enthusiastic about wanting her services, she didn't seem as open to input when it came down to doing the work. Freda was passionate about the mission, and about her desire to make a difference, so she continued to try to convince her Executive Director to try just one idea that she suggested. But she just wasn't open to doing anything different. Yet, she held an expectation that she would have different results simply because she hired a communications person. Freda was brought in to design a more innovative approach, but was given a very narrow lane to

121

operate within. She was able to produce some wins, but she knew that so much more was possible. What began with great excitement, quickly over time, started to wane. Freda became less enthusiastic about the role and, ultimately, started to dread going into the virtual office. After a big showdown around a lackluster campaign (one that the Executive Director created and insisted upon), Freda recognized that change just wasn't possible here. But, for some reason, she just kept holding on. "What sealed the deal for me was my daughter," she shared. "One day, I got off of a Zoom conference call and my daughter asked me, 'Mommie, why do you look so sad all the time when you're on the computer?'" Taking a deep breath, Freda gathered herself, "That was it for me. I was no longer willing to model misery for my children."

This is not an uncommon narrative. Many of us (and I say this with love) pay lip service to change only to slide right back into our comfort zones. The idea of change is alluring, but the reality can be uncomfortable, emotional, and even paralyzing. This is why we begin with exploring your narratives because they will dictate how far you're willing to go to have a new reality.

Freda's courage did pay off. She left—and soon after, launched her own initiative and attracted the perfect client. This organization loved her ideas, put her on a huge retainer, and gave her the freedom to test her theories. The Executive Director's fear-based entrenchment did not. And sadly, that nonprofit organization, and its important work, ultimately shut down.

Before we make a change, some of us need permission. We may not even be aware that it's what we've been waiting for. Like Freda, it took her daughter to share her authentic observation before she felt empowered to move. There's no judgment here, but an important insight about how deep the habit of enduring is. For others of us we need certainty—and this is where it gets sticky, because we may be holding on to some deeply ingrained cultural conditioning about "safety and security" that may not actually be true. Moreover, it may cause us to create even bigger obstacles to our own success.

To transform these habits, we have to meet them with compassion. None of us wants to stand still. We all seek to evolve and grow. This is one of the biggest points of contention around our Resignation. Even when we drill into the money, for many people, the growth in revenue equates to progress and achievement. It's one of the many ways we've been taught to measure our success.

But growth and comfort do not typically co-exist. You must have some skin in the game. And where it may have been easy to hand over certain decisions (i.e. point the finger) to somebody else, we've got to be willing to take the lead from here on out.

Our success is now 100 percent our business.

The moment we start Renegotiating is the moment we say yes to having greater agency and authority in our lives. Now, this doesn't mean you're always in control, because the world is vast, and there are many factors operating in any given scenario. But what it does mean is that you have a voice and an intentional part to play in how it goes. It also means that as you move into greater alignment with your truth, there are natural laws that begin to activate and go to work on your behalf.

If you are a person of faith, these principles still apply. However, you choose to define your source; it is now between you and that

123

all-providing energy to chart your path. Whether it's partnering with the laws of spirit or the laws of nature or the laws of science, it's a co-creative process from here on out.

If you are revved up and ready to go, that's awesome! Because then it's just a matter of consistent aligned choices and actions associated with the new reality. You begin the pursuit, you invite the support, you prioritize the time, and you are on your way.

But, if you find that you can't even get out of the gate, then it's time to take a deeper look at what's operating.

How *Do* I Change My Mind?

It begins with your awareness; you need to know which narratives are keeping you stuck. In the Reclaiming process, I asked you to take an inventory of which stories you wanted to maintain vs. which ones you were ready to let go. As you observe the nature of your inner dialogue right now, you may find that a couple of stories you didn't see managed to slip through the cracks, or you may discover that a couple of your *Greatest Hits,* as I like to call them, are still holding on for dear life.

That simply means you've got more Reclaiming to do as you move forward. So your next step is to accept this fact and make a clear decision about that narrative or those narratives. Will you continue to entertain them or are you truly ready for something new?

Once you step back into the process of Reclamation and you rededicate yourself to a new story, we want to ensure that the story you choose actually empowers the change you want to make.

For example, if you've discovered a narrative that says, "If I leave this job, I'm going to starve," then we definitely want to address this fear. As you unpack it, you may find lots of cultural messages instilled from family members around job security. And if you've Reimagined work as a freelancer or entrepreneur or work in a profession that doesn't make the primary list of what's "respectable" or "acceptable," then we can clearly see why you might feel stuck.

So this new narrative has got to speak to this particular challenge in a way that will encourage you to take that next step.

Some examples include:

- "I have many opportunities to share my talents and make great money."
- "The perfect scenario is looking for me, I just need to raise my hand."
- "I believe that I make the most money when I am inspired, so I'm going to follow my inspiration."

You might even need to add "I love my grandpa and ..." to the front of your statement.

This may seem like a subtle shift, but if we hold the people we love at odds with our dreams we will not move. You can work with the previous statements or you can create your own; the goal is to notice which statements actually resonate and invite your nervous system to relax.

Once you have a statement you can work with, put that one on heavy rotation—on your phone with an alarm, on a Post-it note in the mirror, as a screensaver on your laptop. Wherever you are resting your eyes, you have an opportunity to take in this new conversation.

Changing Your Mindset about Change

Once you begin to feel movement (i.e. excitement and energy), with the new statement, you want to turn to your most pressing concern. This is where the Realignment process kicks in. What is currently operating in your life that could pose a threat to your progress? For right now, let's keep this between you and you. What choices, habits, or behaviors are driving you towards more of the same? The more specific you can be here the better.

I want to give you three potential examples so that you can discern which feels most aligned with where you are:

- **Scenario 1:** Let's say that this is less about leaving your job but more about creating a whole new relationship to the organization and the work. Let's just say that you want to advance within your current ecosystem and you're trying to do it in a way that feels more authentic to you. Where are you being invited to realign? Is it around taking better care of yourself so that you can show up more energized around the work? Is it around learning how to advocate for yourself so you can stand for your value? Is it about pursuing a new role within the company that feels more meaningful and purposeful to you? What do you see?

- **Scenario 2:** You know you ultimately want to go out on your own, but you recognize that you're not in a place where you can do it today. Where are you being invited to realign? Maybe it's around developing a plan for how you'll get there with an actual date. Or maybe it's getting clear about how many paychecks you need to stack before you feel confident making the leap. Or maybe it's about identifying the next organizational opportunity that further prepares you for the entrepreneurial road ahead. What do you see?

- **Scenario 3:** You're already on your own but now you're looking to pivot in a new direction. Where are you being invited to realign? Perhaps it could be around your relationships. Maybe certain collaborators have not been doing their part. Maybe certain investments haven't paid off or maybe you need a change of environment and some real space to focus. What do you see?

Once you get clear about your most important considerations, you now have an opportunity to take those vital actions in service to your reimagined vision.

Where Am I Ready for Change?

When it comes to making the necessary changes to support your new vision for success, I've often found that there are two types of people:

- The "back against the wall types"—who need the rug ripped out from under them in order to fly.
- The "belly full" people—who need to ensure that their rent is paid and their dinner is secured before they can focus on the task at hand.

When it comes to taking the necessary steps to reimagine your work, which one are you?

When I'm working with clients who are in the midst of massive change, I always like to share these archetypes and ask them—what do you see? It is important to understand your orientation because it will help you determine where you're most ripe and ready to grow.

The Growing Edge distinction comes from the groundbreaking work of Gail Straub[1] and David Gershon,[2] founders of the Empower Institute. Using the metaphor of organic growth vs. static growth, they invite us to find that sweet spot where there is just enough comfort to fuel our confidence while embodying just enough challenge or stretch to make it interesting.

Where is that sweet spot for you?

Once you find that edge, your job is to take the next step and the next step and the step after that and so on. When it comes to change, you don't have to be grandiose all of the time. Some of the most profound transformations happen through the most subtle shifts and corresponding actions. But sometimes there are times when you just need to peel that Band-Aid off and go for it. Developing a keen sense of awareness around that edge becomes an important new skill to build when Renegotiating.

Changing Your Mind in Community

Though Renegotiating is a unique and deeply personal process for every single one of us, there is tremendous power in being able to do this important work in a supportive community. Having like-minded people around you who are devoted to their own journeys brings a level of encouragement and support that enables us to take those important steps.

One of the things I hear most often from the leaders we serve is how valuable having an accountability structure is: people in their lives who are rooting for them, while also challenging them to work through the necessary obstacles that stand in the way of their newly defined vision for success. Fellow travelers represent a special kind of support because they are on the field with you—drawing inspiration from your courage just as you are drawing inspiration from theirs.

No matter what path you take, your belief in positive change is necessary. As you cultivate a new level of clarity about who you are and what you want, your belief in change can give you the necessary fuel for moving from where you are to where you want to be. Change is not only vital, it is inevitable. But it will be up to you to decide what kind of change you want it to be. Will you give yourself the license to Renegotiate?

Your Terms

1. When it comes to achieving your new vision for success, how open are you to change?

   Rate yourself on a scale of 1–10.

2. As you consider your rating above; can you identify which narratives are moving you forward vs. which ones may be holding you back?

3. When it comes to making the necessary changes within yourself—where do you feel most ripe and ready to grow?

4. As you consider the quality of your community—who have been your greatest supporters? If you notice that community is missing for you—consider one action you might take to enlist greater support.

For more downloadable tools and resources, go to: www.move thecrowd.me/IA-resources.

Chapter 11

Signing Your Own Permission Slip

"No matter who you are or how ambitious you are, in order to move forward you have to be uncomfortable. – You have to take that leap of faith."
—DK, Architect, Sr. Director of a Luxury Brand

When we looked at thwarting in Chapter 3, our lens was set to a pretty wide angle. We had a big-picture, macro perspective: systemic roadblocks, cultural conventions baked into policy, procedure, and practice. I call those 25-foot barriers. They're big, formidable, and definitely have to be dealt with, but they're also external to you—they live and operate in the space of "out there." Yet, when it comes to Renegotiating, sometimes the barriers that prove to be the hardest to overcome are the ones you've internalized "in here." I call these the two-inch barriers, the ones that live inside your head. Whether you installed them yourself or someone did that for you, they're the culmination of everything you've seen, heard, and experienced that has led you to believe "I can't."

Just as we get to challenge ourselves around the degree to which we believe real change is possible, we also get to explore our own sense of entitlement (or lack thereof) when it comes to having the things in our lives and work that really matter. One of the greatest awakenings we've shared through the Great Resignation is the discovery of how much we do or do not feel worthy or empowered when it comes to what *we* value. When we go through challenging times, it can diminish our sense of hope. When we grapple with ingrained structures that seem unwilling to budge, we can question what's possible. When we encounter relationships that are driven by wounded and wounding ambition, we can opt out of trusting people altogether.

Long before we ever meet an obstacle, we can be working up a sweat in our minds—getting ready for battle. We become convinced of how it will go and we reject ourselves or the situation long before anyone else can. Our inner guardian (protector) kicks into overdrive curbing our enthusiasm and talking us off the ledge. It is masterful at denying—offering one compelling excuse after another about why our aspirations are out of bounds. Even if we can wrap our minds around the fact that it is indeed possible as in physically feasible; we still have a ways to go before we can embrace the potential that it's possible for *us*!

Those two-inch barriers are stubborn. You know the ones: I have a mortgage to pay! I have kids to feed! Who do I think I am? I don't come from privilege! They would never let me do *that*. If all the generations of my family couldn't do this, why should I think I can? My mother/father/whoever would never speak to me again!

We must dismantle the internal obstacles that result in denying yourself permission to do what you feel called to do. Our work here starts with confronting the degree to which this often unconscious nay-saying is enabling your unhappiness and allowing yourself to consider—just *consider!*—that these messages might not be your friend and that as much as you believe they are keeping you safe and secure, they may actually be stunting your growth.

It can be easy to be seduced into following the pack; but we know where that path leads and we've already been there and done that (thank you, Resignation). So now it's time to discover what is *our way*. How does our reimagined life and world of work become our reality?

Oh, Yes You Can!

One of my favorite thought exercises to use with clients who stubbornly cling to "I can't" is this scenario:

> Suppose I invite you to lunch, and you say sure, you'd love to. Then I tell you it's going to cost you two hundred and fifty dollars. "Two hundred and fifty dollars! Are you crazy? What do I look like? For two hundred and fifty dollars I could feed myself for a month!" Then I tell you it's lunch with Oprah Winfrey, and only 10 people will be there. "Oh!" you say, "When do you need the money?"

Everyone gets that story, and it really does start to open eyes and hearts and minds with its lesson that if you really want to, then yes, you really can. You can imagine how, even if $250 were equivalent to two months' rent, you would find a way to come up with the money, *if it were important to you.* Cutting back here, delaying a planned purchase there, and so on. What's more, you can imagine how you'd do whatever it took to manage the logistics of the lunch—finding a sitter for your kids or your diabetic cat, arranging for someone to cover your shift at work, figuring out how to get from wherever you are to whatever amazing restaurant Oprah picked. And don't even get me started on all the effort that would go into what you'd wear!

The bottom line is when it's really important to us, we find a way. I don't say this to negate our challenges. I say this to encourage our creativity and our strength. We are far more capable than we give ourselves credit for.

Sometimes asking the world to reinforce our limitations is actually not a contribution. When we find ourselves over the edge and drowning in our fears, doubts, and concerns, the knee-jerk thing to do may be to call off the pursuit, but if we dig deep down, there is a part of us that aspires to move beyond our current state, even when we feel that inner guardian fighting to preserve our status quo. This is not about forcing a situation. It's about finding that *compelling* reason and that ripe and ready opportunity that moves you one step closer.

Change, progress, opportunity, success—these are all a function of belief. Do you believe in yourself? Do you believe in your vision? Do you believe in your talents and abilities? These are not rhetorical questions. Most of us would reply, "Yes, but …." Take a moment and ask yourself, Whose permission are you waiting for?

That fabulous lunch is what could happen if you were willing to challenge your two-inch barriers. That amazing new role in an awesome company could happen if you were willing to believe that it exists—not just in theory, but for you. That phenomenal new client could find you if you were willing to get the word out on who you are and what you're offering.

You just need to give yourself permission—or rather five key permissions.

The Five Permissions

Any place where we feel unentitled or unworthy is a place where we're likely to sell ourselves short. Beyond all of the complaints and rationalizations are the fears and concerns that crave to be addressed. In my experience there are five key permissions that support increasing our sense of agency and belonging (fulfillment). They are permission to be clear, permission to pursue, permission to be on the journey, permission to succeed (or fail) on your terms, and permission to be supported.

Permission to Be Clear

Now that you've done the awesome work of reclaiming your stories, realigning your values, and reimagining what your life and work could be—honor it! Your clarity about who you are and what you want is what gives you the power to say "yes" or "no" in any situation. When you give yourself permission to be clear, you release the habit of "going through the motions" or operating as if you have no choice. You are no longer at the mercy of your circumstances. You give up being a prisoner to what everybody else thinks you should do. You take responsibility for your vision and your values; you acknowledge it, speak it, you engage around it—you claim the vision as rightfully yours.

When you give yourself permission to be clear, you're letting go of the fog and the need to manage everybody else's confusion too! You're embracing what is so for you in a way that encourages others to do the same.

Permission to Pursue

Once you're clear about what you want, it's time to *act* on your clarity—to bring consistent, aligned effort that moves you toward your ambitions. It's not enough to just *have* them. This is about owning your right to go for it wholeheartedly and give it your all. This is the exciting part! (Yep, and the scary part too!) But know that every step you take in the direction of our new vision matters. You may find that this is one of the hardest permissions to grant because of all the other constraints of your day-to-day. This is where you get to confront and transform the habit of deprioritizing yourself and the things that matter *to you*.

For some of you, there is no issue at all with going for it—you've got this! But, it may be more about the nature of *how* you pursue—in your reimagined world of work—what's different? If all out pursuit is a challenge, where are you holding back? Or denying yourself the call to a bigger vision? Can you give yourself the opportunity to achieve something that really matters in a way that feels authentic and values aligned? When you give yourself permission to pursue, you're saying I'm worthy and what I want is worthy too.

Permission to Be on the Journey

This involves genuinely embracing the idea of being a work-in-progress. It means being okay with imperfection and being willing to learn as you go—and not just learn, but unlearn too in order to co-create, evolve, refine, and mature. It may be a little messy at first, the key here is to meet yourself with encouragement and compassion.

This is where you transform the habit of needing to be perfect, which is exhausting and often unattainable. Being on the journey means you recognize that the life and work you've reimagined will require you to show up over and over again—as a devotional practice. That this new form of success you're seeking is less about a destination and more about a way of being. It will ask you to bring a beginner's mind—even if you're a veteran. It will inspire you to reach higher with no guarantees. It will remind you that you may stumble, and fall and fail, before you learn how to walk in these new shoes.

Being on the journey means you get to heal and let go of the past. You get to make peace with the mistakes that have haunted you—as you invite the potential to make new ones as you move. It also means being willing to see setbacks as learning experiences. You get to (re)discover yourself and what you desire in a whole new way. With every step you take, you get to see your progress and believe that great things are happening for you.

Permission to Succeed (or Fail) on Your Terms

For some of us, no matter what we attempt, success is never a question. But for many more, there is this lingering feeling, always hanging out in the background that makes us consistently brace ourselves for what could go wrong (failure and disappointment). As you think about your reimagined reality, I'd like you to ask yourself: *Have you given yourself permission to succeed?* This is about letting the good be good without disparaging or undermining yourself or your success. It means embracing your wins as wins and even, dare I say, celebrating them. It means believing that your hard earned wisdom and intuition will amount to awesome, tangible results with your name on them. It means knowing that even in the face of adversity, that your new definitions and pursuits *will* bear fruit. Permission to succeed is all about giving yourself room to receive the very best that life and work have to offer. When you give yourself permission to achieve what matters, you're giving yourself the right to be fulfilled—on your own terms and by your own definition.

Permission to Be Supported

This is a hard one for many of my clients, partly because of the pervasive American myth of rugged individualism, partly because so many of us have become so siloed. But this only makes it more critical. Success doesn't happen in a vacuum—nobody does it alone. You have to know what you need in order to thrive, you have to believe that you can ask for support and receive it, and you have to be willing to work unapologetically to put that support in place. Having amazing support can mean the difference between achieving your desired reality and having all the reasons why it didn't manifest. When you give yourself permission to be supported, you demonstrate to the world and to yourself that "this matters!" Imagine what would be possible if you saw every person and every situation as a contribution to your success. Whether they reinforce your clarity or fuel your pursuit, let people love you, contribute to you, acknowledge you, and invest in you in ways that are expansive and game changing.

On the Road to Permission

I remember the first time I met Annalee, she was super quiet and shy. She'd just transitioned out of a huge corporate role and was taking some time off to rest and regroup. She'd just given birth to her second child and making the decision to leave her coveted role in a male-dominated industry was not an easy one.

> "The first permission I had to give myself was permission to leave." Once she left, she decided to do something even more radical, and give herself a break—time to be a mother, full-time and on her own terms. "Permission #2!," she says. As we delved into her history, I learned that she was chewing on a new idea, one that would support

high-achieving moms who were often torn between their professional ambitions to lead and their personal ambitions to mother. "I think the two are connected," she said, "but there are very few places where women can speak openly and honestly about the challenges of each without feeling like they are being judged." Tell me more, I encouraged. As Annalee began to share more in depth around her own experience and the conversations she'd been having with other moms, I was fascinated. When I asked her if she intended to work on the idea, she immediately shied away, "Who me?" she said. "Yes, you!"

As we explored the potential of coaching she shared, "This is a really big deal for me—considering the possibility of investing in myself in this way." That would be permission #3. Six weeks after our initial conversation she reached out. "I've decided to give myself the next year to work on this."

In our first session, she shared about how risky it felt to pursue this desire and to put real resources behind it. "It's one thing to talk about it you know over dinner with another couple, but to actually say 'I'm going to do this' and explore what it could look like if I offered this space to other women feels very provocative to me—especially as an immigrant and woman of color (WOC). We don't get these options very often." As we begin to map out the vision and start to create a timeline for how she might engage others in the idea, all kinds of road blocks begin to emerge. "What will my family think?" was a big one. "Will I be seen as credible? Is this industry of mothering even legitimate?" was another. In the face of these persistent challenges Annalee finally realized that—to be of service to other women—she needed to reclaim the value of her

Signing Your Own Permission Slip

own motherhood and the work of mothering. As an ambitious WOC, she decided to give herself time to mother full-time and on her own terms. Permission #4!

At every turn, Annalee faced yet another fear or concern that threatened her ability to move forward. And one by one, I witnessed her courage as she just kept giving herself more and more permission. As she arrived at each session, with the next internal barrier, our work became clear: to break through and transform them—one by one. As we continued to nurture the idea, her voice became more powerful, my homework assignments became more radical, and this unique offering for high-achieving moms became more and more clear. Through the practice of permission she went from articulating the vision to spending crucial time speaking with moms, and learning more about the challenges and gifts of their realities, what they wanted, what they felt like they needed, and what formats would serve them most. She took these insights into her own laboratory and began to design popup moments rooted in her unique insights.

Step by step, she moved intentionally and compassionately towards the next goal. Sometimes the call was to create something out in the world, and sometimes the call was to work through yet another internal barrier that would enable her to hold space for her own journey. With every moment of fear, or challenge, she responded with great compassion and from that compassion came more permission and with each layer of permission, came the next level of clarity, conviction, and pursuit. She is currently continuing to nurture the dream, working on her next offering. She is excited and terrified but her permission practice is strong. Her vision is clear and she is gaining recognition and supporters along the way. "I'm clear that I'm just learning how to be more of myself," she said, "learning how to be comfortable and happy in this skin."

In case you haven't figured it out yet, the only person who can give you this kind of permission is you! Permission is an act of self-honoring and self-love. It is a practice that we cultivate in service to our process of Renegotiation. It is the skin we put in the game in honor of the people we most aspire to be and in support of the work we most want to do in the world. It does not have to be lofty and it doesn't have to happen overnight. The more we allow ourselves to be in our truth, the more we invite the very opportunities and resources we need to achieve our vision and honor our new definitions. With greater permission we get to discover the true nature of our ambition, which is the next step in our process as we prepare to re-enter our world.

Your Terms

1. As you explore the five Permissions, take an inventory of which ones feel most vital to your Renegotiation. Notice, where is permission present? Where is it missing?

2. Where permission is missing, ask yourself, What would it look like to grant yourself permission in those key areas? Get as specific as you can. For example, if you gave yourself *permission to pursue*, what specifically would you be doing that you're not doing right now?

(continued)

Signing Your Own Permission Slip

(continued)

3. Use the template I provide in the resources section (https:// movethecrowd.me/IA-resources) to fill out and sign your own permission slip! Post that slip in a prominent area where you can see it. Any time you feel challenged along the way, read this slip out loud and remember—you have all of the permission you need to take the next step towards your desired reality.

For more downloadable tools and resources go to: www.move thecrowd.me/IA-resources.

Chapter 12

Cultivating Your True Ambition

"Whether you want something big or you want something small, you want. And maybe that's the thing that we have trouble with. How do I let myself want what I want—and let that be the highest goal?"

—VC, Thought Leader, Mom, Entrepreneur

As you begin to adopt a new mindset about change and give yourself more permission to have what you really want, you will become more optimistic about what's possible. And when you become inspired about what's possible, you have the potential to forge a whole new relationship with your ambition. This is the next crucial step in Renegotiating.

Rather than wanting what everyone else wants, you get to want what *you* want. Rather than feeling like you have to exploit and control everything and everyone, you get to consider how you can use your greatest talents and ideals to create even more good. Rather than sacrificing your mental and emotional well-being, you get to do that good on your terms with more peace, more ease, and more joy.

Remember in Chapter 6 when I introduced you to the five aspects of wounded ambition? Now we'll explore how to redeem those wounds and get to a place of what I call *true* or *intentional ambition*. We'll see what it looks like to discover our deepest aspirations and pursue them in a way that honors our most authentic selves and our vision for a better world—even if that world is just our family or neighborhood.

This brings me to a beloved client of mine, Marlee. Marlee is an esteemed senior leader in the field of Higher Education.

> "If you asked me if I was ambitious just five years ago, I might have denied it. Though I think I've always been motivated to achieve, I never really felt like it was okay to say it, especially as a woman," she paused, "I thought that people would think I was pushy or cutthroat. So I never really made my desires known."

> "But something changed for you in the last 5 years. What is it?" I asked.

> She leaned forward, "I think *I've* changed. During the last five years, I've actually done so much in my role as a leader and in my life as a mother and both have inspired me to embrace more of who I am, which includes my motivation to succeed. Before, success for me was mostly about achievement, which was connected to a specific title or specific role and now, it's connected to the difference I'm making with my students, or to the health and well-being of my boys. I've had some great role models who have shown me how to embrace these new definitions and desires. And I feel proud of where I am and where I'm going."

When your aspirations align with: (1) being your best self, (2) making your highest contribution, and (3) benefiting others, you are in the realm of true ambition. True ambition recognizes that every single one of us matters and has a valuable contribution to make—one uniquely suited to our distinct nature and talents. It also recognizes that when we are able to make our highest contributions, we move towards a better world, a world where more people get to thrive and achieve *their* full potential.

Five Wounds and Five Redemptions

The five aspects of true ambition are designed to invite greater love, joy, peace, and liberation. I call these five aspects *redemptions* because they have the potential to transform old, wounded ways of being and create a more expansive, inspirational, and regenerative way of living and working. As we shift from old-paradigm, zero-sum strategies driven by greed, dominance, and exploitation, we have the potential to discover a new level of generosity, stewardship, and collaboration—by-products of a more loving and compassionate way of achieving.

Redemptive ambition invites us to become deep listeners, collaborative (and proactive) problem solvers and accountable citizens. Each redemption correlates to an aspect of wounded ambition—or, to put it more succinctly, to a wound—but is also its own stage in a progression toward becoming a more authentically realized human being.

Figure 12.1 shows my true ambition framework that replaces the behaviors of old paradigm with the behaviors of true and intentional ambition.

Table 12.1 describes each of the five redemptions.

TRUE AMBITION FRAMEWORK™

WOUNDED AMBITION OLD PARADIGM (5 Wounds)		TRUE AMBITION™ NEW PARADIGM (5 REDEMPTION)
Imposter Syndrome	⟶	Courageous Imperfection
Righteous Competition	⟶	Enlightened Humility
Lack of Ownership/Disenfranchisement	⟶	Sacred Embodiment
Playing Safe/Playing Small	⟶	Unapologetic Devotion
Hiding Out/Being Invisible	⟶	Shining Bright, Standing Tall

Figure 12.1 True Ambition Framework.

Cultivating Your True Ambition

Table 12.1 Five Wounds and Their Redemptions.

Wound	Redemption	Description
Imposter syndrome: an inability to see ourselves and recognize our true value	*Courageous imperfection*	Rewrites the narrative that says we must be perfect to be loved and accepted, that our value is measured by the degree to which others are pleased. *Courageous imperfection* says I am here, I matter and I'm willing to pursue my calling—even if it's messy, even if everyone doesn't love it, even if it makes me vulnerable and open to critique. It recognizes the value in the things we attempt with the best intentions and encourages us to risk being real instead of perfect.
Righteous competition: obsession with being better than everybody else	*Enlightened humility*	Rewrites the narrative that says our inherent value lives in the egoic acquisition of knowledge—that we are what we know and that cultivating a know-it-all superiority complex is something to aspire to. *Enlightened humility* believes that knowledge is power to be used to facilitate rather than dominate. It says I know some things for sure, but I don't know everything. It honors natural curiosity and the awe and wonder we experience when we get to engage with the knowledge and wisdom of others. It carries a deep appreciation for collective wisdom and the opportunity to constantly grow and evolve. It honors the truth of our equality and appreciates the unique and varied contribution of others.
Lack of ownership/disenfranchisement: a denial of self and others	*Sacred embodiment*	Rewrites the narrative that says that there is not enough and that vulnerability and transparency make us weak. It invites us to see all aspects of who we are: the good, the challenging, the strong, and the undesirable. To take responsibility for our gifts and our struggles. To take full ownership of our wants, needs,

Wound	Redemption	Description
		desires, and actions. To be accountable for where we cause harm and apprecia-tive of where we do good. *Sacred embodiment* believes that there is enough and that we are enough and the more we are at peace with ourselves the less we need to be negatively concerned about the access or advancement of others.
Playing safe/playing small: a tendency to gravitate toward "coasting"	*Unapologetic devotion*	Rewrites the narrative that says what your heart desires doesn't really matter because it's all about what pays the rent and what is expected of you. It evokes your passion, values, gifts, and highest abilities, it's the call to your *dharma* (i.e. your true nature and highest expression) and to the path that holds the greatest level of reward. It's the invitation to invest in the things that you value in the name of greater joy, freedom, and fulfillment. *Unapologetic devotion* draws on the things you're willing to stand up and make an effort for—your principles and convictions, your ideas and innovations for the people you love and the world you envision.
Hiding out: the tendency to shy away from the spotlight promoting the voices, visions, and ideas of others	*Shining bright, standing tall*	Rewrites the narrative that says that it's not okay to shine and that being in the spotlight (literally and metaphorically) is dangerous. It celebrates our innate desire to be seen, heard, and acknowledged. It invites us to take up space and take our rightful place. It urges us to make our unique and vital contributions—our voice, vision, ideas, and innovations. *Shining bright, standing tall* encourages us to embrace the love and recognition for who we are and for what we do with grace and gratitude.

Cultivating Your True Ambition

The Journey from Wounded to True

We've all had moments in our lives and in our work where we've shown up as less than our most powerful selves. However, as we become more internally aligned with our most authentic selves, the five redemptions become integral to how we Renegotiate. As we define and set out to achieve success on our own terms, we gravitate toward new desires and motivations. When we examine the six frontiers that supported our Realignment work in Chapter 8, we can now ask: What are the conditions and factors that enable us to show up as our best selves? What are the conditions and factors that allow us to make our highest contributions?

This brings me to Talia's journey. Talia is a C-suite executive who chose to reboot her career at the height of the pandemic.

> "I was someone who was incredibly ambitious. With any role or position, it was my mission to outwork everyone around me." Talia learned how to do this from her mother who she said was a natural born leader, who worked a full-time job and raised three kids. "She never stopped, never sat down, and I just assumed that was what was expected of me." When Talia took on a big international role, it was understood that she would work around the clock to produce the desired results. "We set lofty goals, and as a woman at the head of it all, I knew I had a lot to prove." However, when she arrived at her new post, she had no idea how bad it was. There were so many disconnects between the mission and reality. "Morale was in the toilet and I was inundated with complaints." Talia worked day and night to turn it around. She pushed and stretched, advocated and lobbied, appeased and cajoled all in an

attempt to make it work. All she could think about was the fact that she could not let this fail and that if it failed, she would only be proving those nay-sayers right.

"To say that I burned out is an understatement. When I decided to leave, I knew that it had to be different. When word got out that I'd left, I was courted by a number of major brands—they were offering me a lot of money—but I just couldn't bring myself to say yes to any of them. I could just feel in my bones that it would be more of the same. I took some time away, and during that time, I just kept asking myself, 'What do you really want to do? And what would it look like for you to do this work *your* way?' As I posed these questions to myself, I recognized that I had a passion for supporting teams who struggled with the same challenges I found in my last role. What would be different is that I'd only work with leaders who were deeply invested in making those necessary changes. By asking myself these questions, I began to develop a whole new set of criteria for my ideal company. Instead of focusing solely on title and salary, I became passionate about understanding the company's mission, the values of its leaders, and the quality of its resources. My focus shifted from trying to convince them that I was good enough to trying to assess if they were indeed right for me. In my almost 20 years of organizational experience, I'd never done this level of due diligence. It felt amazing to be in an interview process where I was having real conversations, with real stakeholders. I wasn't looking for perfection; I was looking for commitment. Took me a while, but I finally found the right opportunity. Every morning I wake up now, I'm energized, I feel like I'm being encouraged to

Cultivating Your True Ambition

do exactly what I said I wanted to do from the very beginning. We've had lots of curveballs thrown our way. But the commitment is strong, real trust has been built, and we're making progress every single day. My primary motivation is to empower these teams and to work in ways that enable me to bring greater joy and balance to my own life and to the work we're doing."

The journey from wounded to true begins with awareness and is sustained by an intentional commitment to live and work in ways that inspire and enliven us—and in ways that motivate and inspire others. It will require patience. It will command us to make conscious choices. It will encourage us to show up in ways that increase our capacity to contribute even more to the missions and ventures that captivate and challenge us in the best possible ways.

When we step into any environment, we can now begin to assess what feels in integrity. With every interaction we can become more intentional about how we initiate and how we respond.

We learn through observation about what triggers our old, ingrained reactions vs. what invites and encourages our new beliefs and commitments. As we bring more of our true selves to the table we become more clear about who we are and where we belong.

Our reimagined way of aspiring and achieving will require dedication. On any given day we may find ourselves bouncing back and forth between the old and the new. Any time we find ourselves slipping into a negative status quo, our job is to take a step back, meet it with compassion, and then make a new choice. In those moments, we get to ask ourselves: Who do I aspire to be at this moment? What feels in integrity with my values? What will really make a difference here for me, for the mission, for the people involved?

Utilizing the redemptive qualities of our ambition, we can intentionally choose Courageous Imperfection, which invites a sense of spontaneity, excitement, and experimentation; Enlightened Humility, which honors what we know while inviting other brilliance to the table; Sacred Embodiment, which encourages greater vulnerability and transparency around the process and accountability around the results; Unapologetic Devotion, which fuels our efforts and reminds us of our mission and what's really important; and finally, Shining Bright, Standing Tall, which allows ourselves and others to be seen, honored, and recognized for their efforts.

Now that we've done the internal work of Renegotiation, it's time to bring our new or newly refined commitments, terms, and conditions out into the world.

Your Terms

1. Take a look at your ambition inventory from Chapter 6, now take a look at the five Redemptions highlighted in this chapter—which redeeming aspects resonate most with you?

2. Over the next two weeks, use Figure 12.1 to observe what's driving your ambition in the day-to-day. Notice what moves you from one side to the other; write about this.

3. When you consider your reimagined vision for work, how might these five Redemptions influence your new terms and conditions?

For more downloadable tools and resources, go to: www.movethecrowd.me/IA-resources.

Part V

How to Renegotiate with Others

Once you become clear about your reimagined vision for work and the true nature of your ambition, it's time to reclaim, re-align, and reimagine (i.e. re-educate and train) with the world around you. Your internal Renegotiation process is designed to help you arrive at a whole new level of clarity and conviction about who you are and what you desire most and to give you the tools to continue to revisit that clarity as you begin to re-engage with the world.

Informed by your new terms and conditions, it's time to cultivate a new context and game plan for how you re-enter your world. This part will help you design how to approach your Renegotiation process with others as well as deepen a unique set of skills aimed at creating more room and space for you to show up in the world as your authentic self. Just as the Renegotiation process encourages you to see yourself newly, it invites the same opportunity for every interaction you have with those in your current reality as they may be renegotiating too!

This will be a frontier of new discoveries as well as affirmations about the things that feel tried and true. New relationships and op-portunities will come toward you while others will either realign in honor of the new paradigm or fall away. The intention of our process for reentry is to give you the opportunity to practice (facilitating) what you desire in your Reimagined world on a daily basis.

Guided by the principles and values that move you toward your realigned and reimagined aspirations, you have the ability to intentionally influence the world around you in a way that feels more inspiring, empowering, and true.

Chapter 13

Setting Up Your Game Plan (and Guardrails) for Reentry

"I always thought I had to struggle to succeed, then I got sick, and working to exhaustion was no longer an option ... success became phenomenal for me when I (re)defined it for myself."

—GSR, Entrepreneur & Celebrity Influencer

Let's say you've done all the work in this book and you're making great progress in moving toward the life of your dreams. Even if you haven't had the luxury of a full sabbatical, your realignment process has (or is) happening. You've also given yourself the room to articulate a clear vision for your desired reality and you're moving toward it. Yes, there have been some bumps in the road, for sure, but by and large you're on your way.

Now, you're ready to ramp it up and re-engage with the most vital parts of your world. Maybe you're returning from taking time away, maybe you're transitioning into a new role, or maybe you've shifted locations and you're now charged with the task of rebuilding your community.

As we examine the state of our world guided by our realigned inventory: What's our top priority? What new values or ethos do we need to become more explicit about? What are the most important practices, protocols, and behaviors we want to be implementing? What are the most important conversations we need to have with the people in our lives and our work?

Just as we've been very intentional about our internal Renegotiation process, we want to bring that same energy to how we re-enter and Renegotiate with our respective realities (with others).

Allow Me to Reintroduce Myself

Though it's not my intention to continue espousing the wisdom of the great Jay-Z, in this case his "Public Service Announcement (Interlude)" is a really valuable one. The honored practice of reintroducing yourself—especially in old environments—can be a very powerful strategy for setting a new context and creating new rules of engagement. Whether you're navigating your most intimate relationships or you're working with your professional team, when you make big shifts, it's important to give your fellow travelers a heads up!

Re-entering an old space with new assumptions can be a recipe for tensions and disconnects. It's up to you to communicate what's different in your reality so that your fellow life and workmates can update their operating systems accordingly. Now, that doesn't automatically mean *they're* going to change. But it does create the potential to reconsider any existing terms and shared agreements—which is exactly what you want.

So, how do you prepare? I highly recommend revisiting the core tenants of the *five redemptions* in Chapter 12 before you dive in—just so that you're not beating people over the head with your "new and improved version"—because that kind of defeats the purpose.

You still may hit some roadblocks or encounter some resistance to your reintroduction; that's okay. Reintroducing yourself can be uncomfortable for you and for those who've grown accustomed to your representative. However, the more you practice, the more you'll find your confidence and even a sense of passion and excitement as you support your most trusted collaborators with getting on the same page.

Don't feel like you have to share *everything* all at once. Depending upon the nature of your relationship and the setting, you may choose to go deep or you may keep it high level. What *is* important is to examine wherever you find yourself holding back and the degree to which your reluctance is causing you to slip back into old narratives and the same unhappiness.

Does this become an opportunity for greater courage and permission? Or is this simply a place where you feel less invested? If it's an environment that feels less welcoming to your true self or if it's a place where you genuinely don't care, you might consider whether or not this relationship, job, or community is still a fit for you.

When you reintroduce, make it fun and/or meaningful; again, it doesn't have to be dramatic (or it can be as long as you bring fun and flare). The point is that you are signaling both to yourself and to the other that something's different here, even if it's just sharing more of the real you. The intention is to invite deeper authentic connection and greater appreciation for this new moment in your life and work and the potential it creates for everyone involved.

This brings me to another beloved client, Naveen. Naveen is a brilliant organizational leader in the entertainment industry who went through a pretty messy and public divorce from a well-known company. He chose to take a step back after the transition to get clear about his next steps and what he wanted at this stage in his life and work.

During his sacred pause he experienced a number of awakenings around his true passions. He recognized that he wanted to stay in his current industry, but he wanted a role that was more creative. He always loved writing but never had the time to work on his craft; he was passionate about kids, but was way too busy to ever volunteer. He also had to admit that he wasn't necessarily known for his warm and fuzzy demeanor. He'd been taught to develop sharp elbows which he'd found to be quite necessary in his company life. As his reimagined vision for work started to take shape, it emerged as an exciting new creative project. As Naveen considered his strategy, he knew he'd be reaching out to old colleagues and friends. "How do I tell these guys about my idea? They're going to think somebody hit me over the head!" He chuckled, "Who are you, and what have you done with Naveen?, they're going to ask me." He paused. I could tell he was nervous. "Wow, I've really changed." He shook his head. "But I know these guys are going to love the idea and I think they'd be perfect collaborators."

Once you've given the heads up, listen! Be open to receiving feedback. Use it as an opportunity to strengthen your existing connection(s), protocols, and ways of working. All of this moves you and ideally others forward.

Boundaries Are Good (for Me *and* You)

But what if I'm trying to provide updates, make changes, do it differently, but those around me just aren't cooperating? How do

I stay true to my new commitments? You renegotiate some doggone boundaries, that's how!

When renegotiating with others, your boundaries need regular monitoring and maintenance because it's easy to slip into old habits. Maybe you've let toxic people into your orbit. Maybe you've agreed to do work that someone else should be doing. Maybe you've allowed yourself to become gradually overwhelmed and have fallen into old patterns to keep up with it all.

Since it's better not to actually crash into a guardrail if you can avoid it, our work here is to help you establish your own internal warning system. Like the grooves in the road that rattle your bones when your car veers too close to the edge, it's important to look for the telltale signs that *you're* veering. In my experience it often begins with a feeling. Notice how you *feel* when you're beginning to get off track: tired, irritable, distracted, overwhelmed, inpatient, anxious? These are all red flags encouraging you to slow down and take a deeper look.

Your boundary checking process consists of three important steps.

Step 1: What Is the Problem?

First, you need to get clear about what's taking you off track. Is it a relationship, a situation, a recent change to your normal routine? Get still and ask: *What decision(s) have I recently made (or not made) that is giving me this experience?*

For example, when I retraced my steps back to get underneath my own misery during my 2017 meltdown, I can pinpoint the exact moment where I made a decision in three separate instances to get in the middle of something that had *nothing* to do with me. I have a

Setting Up Your Game Plan (and Guardrails) for Reentry

tendency to want to fix things—this is a strong byproduct of my co-dependency and traumatic upbringing. I *love* dames and damsels in distress—and anytime my addiction to fixing gets activated, I know I'm in trouble.

Come back to your feelings and ask yourself to determine when you started feeling this way. As you identify the timeline, take a look at the corresponding conversations and events. Try to pinpoint exactly where you turned left when you should have stayed straight.

Step 2: What Would Solve It?

Next, get clear about what specifically in the current scenario is not working for you—and what would fix it. This means being unflinchingly honest about what's happening. Get still and ask: *What are the specific arrangements, expectations, or agreements associated with that choice or decision that are just not working for me?*

Next ask: *Can it be resolved? What would make a difference—immediately?*

For example, when I asked Petuma from Chapter 7 to dig into the most challenging aspect of what was happening with her teammate she got really clear, it wasn't so much that this person was making mistakes, it was the fact that this person had no intention of ever taking any responsibility for those mistakes—that was the thing that made the partnership unworkable. It was a classic case of lack of ownership and accountability and Petuma knew it wasn't going to work for her. When we considered what would really solve the issue, she felt adamant that the person had to go.

Step 3: Who Do You Need to Renegotiate With?

Finally, you need to determine who you may need to renegotiate with. (Sometimes it's just you!)

Get still and ask: *What specific steps do I need to take in order to get back on track?*

For example, in my case, I needed to just say "no" or stay silent and implement the practice of minding my business. Sometimes, all people need is a listening ear. In the case of Petuma, she had some firing to do, so we worked on the process and strategy for that so it could be done with dignity for her and the other person.

The more honest you can be with yourself, the greater your chances of creating a scenario that will work for you and ideally the other person too. Do you need to reclaim—as in take back your space, voice, or power? Do you need to realign—as in do a values check or assess your time, energy, and resources against the corresponding return on investment? Or do you need to totally reimagine—as in overhaul the existing situation, shift your relationship to the situation, or simply say "Peace out!" and let it go? Whatever the case, sticking up for yourself so you can stay on track is a necessary skill set to support your reentry.

How You Spend Your Days Is How You Live Your Life

To quote Annie Dillard, if you ever want to know what you really care about, just take a look at your calendar. How you spend your time is the greatest indicator of what's important to you. We can pay lip service to anything, but it will always come down to what gets your energy, resources, and attention. This is why the work of

161

internal realignment is so important—because it sets the stage for, you guessed it—external realignment!

When you examine your new (or refined) definition of success and the vision for your reimagined life and world of work, what has shifted when it comes to your priorities? And how is that reflected in your day-to-day? For example, if health and well-being is now a priority like never before—how is that reflected in your calendar? If more quality time with your little ones is top of the list now, where are those blocks of time?

For the next two weeks, try keeping a time log. Whether you create a special log or just use your existing calendar, I'm going to ask you to color code everything you do, both on the job and off. The purpose of this exercise is to show you where you are honoring your priorities and where you may be going off course: making other people's agendas or emergencies or dramas your own, squandering your precious resources of time and energy, or keeping company with people who aren't actually in your corner. (That last one is such a big one. We tell ourselves that even if our support system is dysfunctional, at least it's ours, and it's better than being alone. You guessed it: We're going to challenge this thinking!)

You choose the colors, and determine what the buckets are. The most important part of this exercise is to come up with a designated color for the things that really matter to you. You can even create levels—green for things you're cultivating, blue for things you are revamping or realigning to be more in tune with your vision, and yellow for the things you want to eliminate or delegate—yep this includes aspects of your work!

Take a moment every morning to write down one thing you're going to do that aligns with your vision for yourself. And I'll ask you to spend a few minutes every evening checking in. Did you do the thing you said you were going to do? Or did you let yourself succumb to distractions? (Note: There's a difference between distraction and unexpected opportunity; I'll help you figure this out so you can make the distinction for yourself.) Finally, you'll ask the most important question: How do you feel about how you spent the day?

When you begin to organize your time, energy, and interactions in a way that aligns with your priorities, something magical begins to happen. You become energized, excited, curious, passionate, and focused, and a kind of serendipity starts to take over. This brings me back to unexpected opportunities. When you are moving in concert with your vision, you will attract more of the things you desire into your life and they will show up unexpectedly. The more people who have an opportunity to authentically engage with you, the greater the potential is for these kinds of wonderful moments. Creating space to respond to these opportunities are exactly the kind of things we want to make room for.

As you delve into this exercise, you'll see that to a great extent, a time log is a choice log. This is why some of my clients choose to keep color-coding even after their two weeks are up. But the important thing is to just keep noticing the decisions and choices you make each day. Over time, this will help you get better at making choices. When you veer off course, you'll start to notice sooner, and course-correcting will be easier and quicker.

Each of these renegotiation rituals is designed to help you establish a new foundation, set healthy boundaries, and realign your time, energy, and resources in service to bridging your vision with your day-to-day.

Your reintroduction to others may require you to go back to your original vision so that you're in tune with why you are doing all this life-changing work in the first place.

Your boundary-checking may require some important renegotiating with the important people in your life—family, friends, old and new coworkers. Realigning your calendar may require you to hit the pause button on a big decision so you can determine if the opportunity aligns with your ideal criteria.

With every step, you're making conscious and intentional decisions about what matters to you. And you're renegotiating with others to ensure your vision becomes your new reality. In the next chapter I'll give you an amazing tool to use in the process.

Your Terms

1. Consider an important reintroduction you'd like to make. Get clear about your desired outcome and use the tips in the Allow Me to Reintroduce Myself section to support your preparation.

2. Is there a major boundary you need to set? Use the three-step protocol in the Boundaries Are Good section to help you put your foot down.

3. For the next two weeks, create and work with your color-coded time log. As you check in every evening, just observe where the opportunities to renegotiate are. Keep a running list.

For more downloadable tools and resources go to: www.move thecrowd.me/IA-resources.

Chapter 14

Coming to the Table Prepared

"We are in desperate need of spaces and actions that support genuine human to human connection across real and perceived differences."

—JCG, co-founder B Lab

Now that we've developed a game plan for how we'll enter, it's time to take stock of the conversations we need to have to successfully fulfill the vision for our reimagined world. As we take inventory of whos, whats, and wheres, we may discover there are a litany of conversations we need to have—and a number of places where we're being called to reintroduce ourselves, set healthy boundaries, and renegotiate our time, energy, and focus. As we consider the list, it will be equally important that we lay a new foundation for *how* we'll approach these interactions.

You know what makes people sweat? Asking for what they *really* want. It's why so many people drag their heels when it comes to setting boundaries—because it involves dealing with someone else who (1) may not see things the way you do and (2) has the power to say no to what you're seeking. I can't tell you how many of my clients dread the idea of walking into a room, laying their cards on the table, and waiting to see if those cards are going to be thrown back in their face.

Old-school negotiation suggests that there will be a winner and a loser, or at least a scenario where someone (probably us) will be forced to compromise. In our experience, it's almost never been equal. It's us vs. them, and we're at *their* mercy. And, no matter what they tell us, the other side is (mostly) always looking out for themselves.

Throughout the Great Resignation, people know they want something better but figure they'll never get it, so rather than even trying to negotiate, they walk.

Or if they do attempt to negotiate, they're either holding back or ready with their fists clenched. But here's the thing. If you're really going to renegotiate your life, you're going to have to (re) as in (re) ally negotiate at some point. If not for a raise, then for a better deal on office space. If not with your boss, then with your spouse. And it will all go so much better—and be so much less scary—if you do the right kind of prep work.

It begins with cultivating a new relationship with and definition for the process of real negotiation. When you return to the core values and principles that you now want to guide your life and your work, how might real negotiation work differently for you? Remember, negotiation is simply a process driven tool that can be redesigned and reimagined just like everything else.

Consider the potential of designing a process that:

- Supports you in being open, authentic, and transparent
- Enables you to see the humanity of the person sitting at the table with you
- Includes taking the time to really understand the nature of their reality

- Involves seeing the larger picture and the implications of your interactions on the whole ecosystem versus just your piece of the puzzle

- Enlists the five redemptions to help inform your strategy

- Envisions a win not only for those involved in the negotiation, but for the system, community, and culture as a whole

- Entails modeling a new way of operating that has the potential to influence not only this interaction but the entire constellation of interactions around you.

In this chapter I'm going to introduce you, step by step, to a tool that demystifies this kind of prep work and gives you a framework for approaching any real negotiation from a grounded and intentional place. It's a tool called CPR—no, not *that* CPR—and it builds on an approach used by the Hunger Project, an amazing international organization working toward the sustainable end of world hunger.

I got to know the Hunger Project through my husband, Corey Kupfer, who was an investor in the program in the early 2000s. I was lucky enough to join Corey on a Hunger Project investor's trip to Uganda in 2001. That's where I came across the tool they called P&IR; it stood for Purpose and Intended Results, and they used it for collective intention setting and debriefing.

Corey eventually refined this tool through his work with men to create the protocol he refers to as a CPR: Context, Purpose, and (Intended) Results—which he highlights in his book *Authentic Negotiating*.

I'm a huge fan of this tool. I use it with my clients all the time. I've led collective CPR creation processes with dozens of stakeholders—and solo CPRs with everyone from entry-level employees to big-time

CEOs. Clients have used a CPR to propose a raise, architect a multi-million-dollar deal, lead a merger, launch a product, raise capital—and everything in between. The tool is a game-changer, and my clients love it.

Setting the Context

It starts with creating a *Context* for the interaction. As the saying goes, context is everything. And for interactions—*any* interaction, whether you're prepping for a single meeting or for an ongoing series of conversations—the context comes down to *Who do you want to be?* What mindset, vibe, and energy do you want to bring to the table?

For example, let's say that the work you did in Chapter 13 has made it clear that a conversation with your manager is in order. When you show up for that conversation, *how* do you want to show up? Do you want your context to be *bitter, angry,* and *frustrated?* Or do you want it to be *grounded, powerful,* and *clear?* The choice is all yours. And it really does matter. Because even if you get what you want in the short term, if the confrontation is bitter, angry, and frustrated, that doesn't bode well for the quality of your relationship with said manager in the long term. Your Context sets the foundation for the whole experience.

> I once worked with a fantastic leader named Saundie who was getting ready to go into a real negotiation around her bonus. She'd been given a number that was less than she thought she deserved, and she wanted to talk about it. In our CPR process she worked hard to (1) get honest about her disappointment, (2) muster up the courage to get clear about the raise she *really* wanted, and (3) muster up even more courage to do something about it.

Given all of the above, it was important that she have a Context that would really empower her in her negotiation. I took her through a guided reflection where she could see herself having the conversation. And I asked her: "*How do you want to feel?*" The three words she settled on (it took some honing!) were *passionate*, *strong*, and *deserving*. I asked her to give me her definition for each.

For *passionate*, she said, "I want to feel excited about the opportunity to make more money and to finally get to a level that I believe is aligned with the value that I bring." Meaning, it was important that her excitement and enthusiasm showed through.

For *strong*, she said, "I want to feel empowered by acknowledging that I'm taking the initiative here to change something that's really important to me. Standing up for myself and having a voice about how I'm compensated and rewarded requires being willing to honor myself and see my ability to have an impact." For her, being strong was about owning her voice and recognizing that she could have an impact, especially when it came to advocating for herself.

For *deserving*, she said, "I want to know that I'm worthy not just logically, but I want to feel emotionally worthy of the best that life has to offer, including this increased bonus."

What's important to notice are the narratives that might get evoked by the *feelings* you have going into the negotiation. Traditionally, we've been taught that our feelings have no place in a professional setting, so for many of us, if we can't get past the intense emotions we feel, it becomes really hard to negotiate. Your context setting work *includes* giving yourself room to feel and express as part of your preparation. You may even determine that giving voice to those feelings are important in the negotiation as well. So there may be some additional work to do that will enable you to share your feelings in an authentic way without attacking.

Right now, I just want you to choose one important negotiation from your list. As you select, notice the feelings that arise for you, see them, honor them, and appreciate them. Next, I want you to imagine how you *want* to feel as you're having the conversation. Once you identify the words, take the time to define each one in your own language.

Setting your context means that from the very beginning, you are setting your own terms and conditions and taking the experience into your own hands. You are coming from a place of vision, not victim— exactly where you want to be in any real negotiation.

Aligning with *Purpose*

Next, we'll move on to Purpose. In a CPR there's always a *why*. Why are you engaging in this negotiation? Why does it matter to you? In what specific way does it support your renegotiated vision for your life and your work? In what specific way does it move you forward and create a more positive impact for everyone involved?

Being clear about your purpose is paramount because it helps you determine whether your effort is aligned with where you want to spend your time, energy, and resources.

> My client Jai is a great case study here. Jai had inherited a set of family businesses—multiple entities with lots of stakeholders all moving in very different directions. Getting

everyone on the same page behind his leadership would take significant work, and he wasn't even sure he wanted to *be* the leader. In the past, he'd resisted the responsibility because taking over the family businesses hadn't necessarily been his passion.

So, our Purpose work started with figuring out if the leadership role was even in alignment with his values, time, and resources. (Before you run out into the world, you must get clear within yourself about why you're running!) Once Jai determined that it *was* in alignment—or, through renegotiation, could be—we had to get very explicit about why it mattered, for him and everyone involved. Through our work, he came to see that taking the helm would give him an opportunity to reclaim his capacity to lead—something he'd wanted to do but hadn't believed he could do *his* way. He examined which aspects of the businesses he was really interested in and which he wasn't. He thought about the terms and conditions that would be vital to giving his full yes to this opportunity. And as he began to consider what was truly possible, he started to consider what his vision might yield not only for him but for all the stakeholders and employees.

This is the purpose statement he ended up with: "Taking the helm of this family legacy gives me the opportunity to embrace my own unique talents and gifts as a leader. This opportunity allows me to forge a new chapter of innovation and transformation for these companies, one that brings greater integrity, profitability, and positive impact to every stakeholder involved."

Jai's *why* became so robust that he became positively *energized*. He could see a clear pathway for his contributions and it genuinely excited him. He went from running from an old burden to running toward his new purpose and calling.

When you think about your why, recognize that it's often about more than just this moment. In what way does this conversation or interaction bring you closer to what really matters to you in the long term? With every important negotiation comes the opportunity for longer-term growth and impact. And each interaction has the potential to bring you closer to your vision for your life and your work. As you engage with the people, situations, and circumstances that make up your current reality, it's vital to remain connected to that larger vision and desired impact.

Achieving Your Intended *Results*

The final part of CPR is (Intended) Results—the tangible outcomes you want to achieve. Yours might include securing a 30 percent raise. Or achieving a sold-out show with over 500 people attending. Or signing a deal on the perfect office space to write your new book. You'll have more than one desired outcome (we'll focus on three to five), and they can be qualitative, not just quantitative: Getting to a better working relationship with your partner—through greater listening, deep and authentic sharing, and courageous accountability—absolutely counts too. What's important is that you get super clear about what you really want.

So many people enter into negotiations where they're just not clear about what they want. Or, equally common, they're afraid of giving voice to what they want because they don't believe they're going to get it. Often the result is a waste of energy preparing for a fight that never comes. The truth is, though, not everything has to be a fight.

Slowing down and really giving voice to your desires is one of the greatest ways to ensure you achieve them.

This brings me to my beloved client Ruba. Ruba just landed an incredible executive role with a nonprofit organization working to support Single Mothers with education and job placement. She loved the mission, she loved the team, and was particularly excited about her CEO. They immediately hit it off during the interview and Ruba felt that she could really forward the vision and make an impact. As they entered into the initial stage of negotiations around compensation, Ruba became anxious. When we explored the question of salary and what she wanted, there was no issue, she was clear. The part of the compensation structure that gave her the most anxiety were the requests for team support. Ruba knew exactly what needed to happen to take the mission to the next level, but she also knew that she needed to have a strong dedicated team to make it happen. When she shared this with the HR Director, the woman replied, "No worries! Just tell us what you want." When Ruba went on to try and clarify what she meant by securing a strong team, the HR Director replied again saying, "Yep, got it. No worries! Just tell us what roles you'd need to have filled and we'll make it happen." When we dug into the intended results of Ruba's CPR we used the opportunity to get very explicit about how she desired to design the role and who were the specific players she needed in order to ensure she could implement the desired strategies. As is very common, we needed to unpack her desires so that we could get really clear about each one.

Here's where we landed:

1. **I GET WHAT I NEED TO BE SUCCESSFUL:** My compensation package not only covers my desired salary ($300,000), vacation (six weeks), and benefits (medical and dental), but it also covers my vision for the team and how the work needs to be delineated in order to ensure I'm well supported.

2. **I GET MY DREAM TEAM:** My dream team consists of a combination of two very successful and seasoned designers as well as two super smart up-and-coming project associates. Finally, I have an incredible assistant who manages my calendar and organizes my work in a way that makes me feel totally inspired and energized as I focus on what I do best.

3. **I BECOME MORE CONFIDENT ABOUT NEGOTIATING:** I utilize this amazing new opportunity to courageously ask for what I want and need in order to make my highest contribution to this amazing organization.

Your intended results are just that. Those very specific and measurable outcomes that deliver on your greatest wants, needs, and desires. When you consider your results, also think about what specific area of personal growth this negotiation supports. Through every interaction we have an opportunity not only to achieve more but to become better. To foster greater joy, fulfillment, and freedom for ourselves and those we interact with too.

Important! A Final Word about Preparation

Once you've prepared your CPR, create some time to just sit in silence and review your work. Take it section by section. Absorb the words so that you *feel* totally connected to your Context, your

Purpose, and of course those Intended Results. Before you enter into the conversation, sit in silence again and review. If this is an ongoing negotiation that requires a series of conversations, use your CPR as a ritual to ground and connect before every interaction so that your purest intentions remain front and center.

In addition to your CPR, prepare to come to the table ready to listen. Logically we all understand the importance of listening, but it takes a deep commitment to really be able to take someone else in. One of the most powerful experiences you can ever offer in any negotiation is to lead with listening. When you're fully present with the person in front of you, there's an opportunity to access information that may otherwise be missed if you're more preoccupied with what you're going to say.

Deep listening when practiced consistently becomes deep witnessing. When people feel witnessed they have a tendency to open up in ways they normally would not. As we endeavor to create a new context for our lives and our work, cultivating authentic, transparent, and impactful conversations becomes a skill worthy of mastering.

Use this CPR tool to help you pinpoint and articulate what you really want. Use it to have the conversations that matter with the most important stakeholders in your ever-evolving world. Use it to create an honoring and authentic space where others can enter with the same level of transparency and good will.

In my experience this process produces more than just the outcomes that make it to the page; it often leads to surprising new discoveries, which lead to greater enthusiasm and excitement as the possibility of your reimagined world suddenly starts to become more real.

175

Coming to the Table Prepared

Your Terms

1. Use the CPR process to prepare for an important negotiation drawn from your work in Chapter 13. Create your desired Context, get clear about your larger Purpose, and articulate your Intended Results in a way that is specific and measurable.

2. As you consider each aspect of your CPR, develop your talking points for the conversation in a way that fosters greater authenticity, transparency, and generosity.

3. Consider what additional elements may support a successful interaction. Think about the environment, how you set the stage, your timing—anything that will enable you to have a productive and rewarding conversation.

For more downloadable tools and resources go to: www.move thecrowd.me/IA-resources.

Chapter 15

Overcoming the Scarcity Scare

"Everybody does better when everybody does better."
—Michael Bush, CEO, A Great Place to Work

When I think about all of the renegotiations I've supported (and even some of my own), I recognize that one of the biggest roadblocks many of us face when it comes to putting our cards on the table is our relationship to lack and loss—or more precisely, the *fear* of lack and loss. It can be paralyzing.

Our system of work operates from a mindset of "not enough." It subscribes to zero-sum thinking, which says that a gain for one means a loss for another. In fact, the idea of scarcity is ingrained into every facet of our culture. It also lives at the center of how we understand success. There's only so much to go around, right? And definitely only so much room at the top. This kind of thinking (instinct really) bakes a kind of desperation into our ambition. And it taints our perception of who we have to be in order to succeed. In place of collaboration and connection, the scarcity mindset urges us to splinter and polarize if we want to survive. It is the engine that drives our wounded ambitions and fuels our fears of being left behind.

The scarcity mindset benefits the traditional system of work, especially the traditional corporate (capitalist) system, by breeding fear-based obedience and compliance. And consumerism! In a world of scarcity, more is always better. We can never have enough, even if it means that we have plenty and others have nothing. The scarcity mindset also causes us to do and say all kinds of things that betray our true humanity. This way of thinking, in my opinion, is responsible for the greatest violations of the soul. It has also been the source of our greatest Resignation.

The scarcity mindset is initially imposed on us but soon comes to operate within us, governing the choices and decisions we make. And those choices and decisions have real and often harmful consequences. In the name of scarcity, we endure personal trauma and stand by while others are mistreated; sometimes, depending on our position, we do the mistreating ourselves. We buy into thwarting ideologies and myths that make it impossible for certain people to even earn a living, let alone advance to positions of leadership.

Fortunately, the Great Resignation has been a huge disrupter of the scarcity-based work culture. Many of us are beginning to recognize that we've been holding ourselves hostage to toxic environments and untenable income standards, all in the name of not-enough.

The truth is, there *is* enough. Enough money, opportunity, and dignity to go around. And our willingness to challenge the old stories within ourselves and in our society is what Renegotiation is all about. It will take time and a genuine commitment to loosen the grip of this kind of thinking, but with every interaction, and every real negotiation, it is possible to bring a more expansive, collaborative, and regenerative approach to how we achieve our newly defined and reimagined definitions of success.

Collaboration and Cooperation Are Not New

Though sometimes positioned as novel, the principles of sharing and cooperation are as old as time itself. If you've ever had the privilege of traveling to some of the most remote regions of the world, then you know what it feels like to be transported into a different time and place. As much as we might begrudge the lack of 5G cell and internet service, or the ease and accessibility of Uber Eats, there is something to be said for immersing ourselves in the day-to-day realities of people who live by a different and, dare I say, simpler set of standards.

I remember many years ago traveling to Kenya as part of an international delegation of artists to work on a project called Kilio Cha Haki (A Cry For Justice). It was the brainchild of a brilliant creative producer and activist named Ninka Nauta. Ninka was from the Netherlands but had been working in Kenya for many years focusing on projects that empowered youth. The inspiration for the project came from a desire to make the tools of producing music more accessible to many of the up-and-coming music groups in the townships surrounding Nairobi who didn't have the money to rent the high-priced studios in the city. Armed with a laptop, pro tools, microphones, and a mixing board, Ninka and a team of Dutch producers flew in and set up a makeshift studio in a local township to be able to record the album. I was the only artist invited from the United States. In addition to helping to produce the project the producers trained the local group in the use of the equipment with the intention of leaving everything behind.

We were all crammed into a rundown three-bedroom flat with one toilet and shoddy electricity and plumbing. As word spread about our arrival, artists began to show up in droves. At one point there may have been 15 to 20 of us crammed in that little front room;

our limbs intertwined as we wrote, leaning on walls, and floor-boards for support whenever we could. Meanwhile, others roamed the tiny kitchen in search of bitter tea, working on creating tracks in one bedroom, recording vocals in another, with the final room reserved for those who took quick naps on a sweaty, dingy mattress throughout the night.

I was immediately struck by the way they all welcomed each other, coming from different regions and even different tribes. The cama-raderie felt in the room around making art and saying something important in the process was palpable. This experience of sharing space became even more apparent during dinner time. Armed with a bag of cornmeal, two to three bundles of greens, and maybe, if lucky, a small piece of meat for flavoring, one of the toughest of the bunch, named Anthony, would cook. Tattered plastic plates and bowls would be gathered, chipped teacups, and old pots with no handles were all used to dish out portions of the piping hot food made in a little ancient crockpot. It was some of the best food I ever had in my life! More importantly, everybody ate. They shared plates and bowls, put spoonfuls in their hands, or shared corners of a single plate. When the food was served, you could hear a pin drop, just the low hum of satisfaction accentuated by lips smacking and the occasional spoon scraping up the last bits before clanking down on the surface. There was no tension, no worry, no shoving or forcing, no matter what went in that pot—everyone ensured that no one was left out.

This wasn't just about family—many of these artists did not know one another—there was simply a cultural agreement established rooted in hospitality toward one another that enabled this seamless and organic flow to take place.

As I share this story I wonder if you've had similar experiences. I wonder if these values and principles are inherent in *your* native culture. I wonder if you've felt as if you've had to abandon these more holistic and inclusive principles to pursue a different kind of success and ambition in your Negotiations (aka Navigations).

This debunks the false perception that so many of us have about the "modern world" and the relationship between having "enough" and being willing to share. The sense of deprivation we feel has very little to do with money. This is not to say that money is not important, but it is not everything.

As with money, our work in this world is important, but it is not everything. And it is that lack of balance that often causes the pain and disappointment we feel. The need to cling to things, to control outcomes, to dominate people. When we put that kind of "end all be all" pressure on our work (or anything for that matter), we are liable to suffer. Money and work in their proper perspective are amazing. Money and work operating within the context of a larger vision for your life and your desired expression and contribution to the world are the ultimate gifts.

Though our world is rapidly changing, and not always for the better, there are regions of the world where the values and ethos I've described are alive and well. Whether they've been identified as blue regions or simply coined as paradise, they exist. They even exist in some of the most unlikely places, such as places that have been ravaged by war, corruption, and devastation. People look out for one another in these parts of the world too. And they take that responsibility very seriously.

Not One, But Three Bottom Lines

Just as there are cultures in various regions of the world that practice the values of simplicity, generosity, and inclusivity, there are sectors within the business world that actively aspire to live by the values of responsible stewardship that include people and planet as well as profit. This triple bottom line concept (TBL or 3BL) was coined in 1994 by John Elkington, an esteemed writer and business consultant, to offer a new accountability framework for business performance that extended beyond the traditional (capitalistic) single bottom line focus on shareholder profit.

Through this framework, Elkington invited *and* challenged corporations to play an active role as engaged citizens in the worlds they occupied. This philosophy acknowledged the importance of being accountable not only to shareholders but also to those who are impacted by the company's actions—employees, clients, neighbors, suppliers, etc.—dubbing them as *stakeholders*. These are people who not only have a vested interest in the company's success, but who are also deeply impacted by its methods.

This philosophy adds the planet as an additional stakeholder, acknowledging the very real and significant impact that business has on its immediate and extended physical environment. The aim was to set a new standard for performance that transcended the fixation on revenue growth at all costs and encouraged a commitment to the broader context of social, environmental, and economic sustainability as the ultimate measure for success.

Since Elkington's bold invitation 30 years ago, this triple bottom-line framework has been embraced to various degrees by multinational corporations on down to mom and pops in local economies. This ethos challenges the notion of zero sum at the very core and boasts the impact of pioneering organizations and brands that have led the way, like The Body Shop, (Paul) Newman's Own, the Virgin Group, Ben & Jerry's, Patagonia, Chobani Yogurt, and many others as a demonstration of what's possible.

In 2006 an organization founded by Jay Coen Gilbert, Andrew Kassoy, and Bart Houlahan formalized a new corporate class to reflect the ethos of TBL called a B Corp. It was through their experiences with traditional capitalism and their work in the social entrepreneurial sector where they witnessed and supported those actively working to create more humane ventures that inspired them to launch B Lab and subsequently create the B Corp designation.

Building on the momentum of this legacy, in the fall of 2015 the United Nations created a set of sustainable goals that speak to everything from ending poverty to transforming inequality and strengthening education—17 goals all aimed to be achieved by 2030. As of February 2024, there are over 8,200 B Corporations in 96 countries operating in over 160 industries.

As you already know from our work in Chapter 3, systemic change is the most challenging because it requires deep seeded cultural shifts rooted in new ways of thinking, being, and operating. But the power of this framework is its ability to encourage us to *think and act* differently about what may be possible when we consider the potential of business to be a force for good.[1,2]

The Authenticity, Vulnerability, and Transparency Generation

When we look at the evolution of mainstream values and the challenging of zero sum through the lens of a generation, we can point to a long legacy of agents of change who have laid the foundation for a more just, harmonious, and sustainable economy and world. Though some might relegate their passion for bucking the status quo to a function of their youth, the truth is that Generation Z comes by its ethos, standing on the shoulders of many who have come before.

From the Baby Boomers' protests of the Vietnam War and the fight for Justice and Equity to Generation X's moving of counter-creative cultures like Punk and Hip-Hop from the margins to the mainstream, to the Millennials commitment to sustainability and an ethos of conscious consumerism in a shared economy, all have provided the building blocks for the authenticity, vulnerability, and transparency generation that is Gen Z.

Generation Z's radical sharing mentality was born out of movements and innovations designed to foster greater purpose, accountability, and opportunity. Their ambition is rooted in a desire to be inspired and to live a life of their own creation. They value community, diversity, and cooperation. They share their salaries, their strategies, their ideas, their work; and they seek nonhierarchical leadership in their workplaces. Gen Z also desires to be valued for their technological savvy and innovation while being well compensated, and they either choose or challenge their work environments to align with these values.

In a 2024 Deloitte study on Gen Z and Millennials in the workplace they found that for Gen Zers 86 percent stated that having a sense of purpose is very to somewhat important to them. This same study also found that 44 percent of these contributors would not even consider roles in companies whose personal ethics did not align with their own. Fifty-five percent reported they and their colleagues are putting pressure on their employers to take action regarding climate change.[3]

Gen Z moves with the desire for a kind of freedom and autonomy that can feel intimidating to traditional structures. They also carry a unique perspective around their work ethic and the balance of work–life integration. They believe that whole life equals whole success, which is where we might be inspired to take a page. Granted, they *are* challenged to build greater skills in emotional intelligence, decision-making, and real negotiation. But that creates a powerful opportunity for mentorship as we seek to reimagine what an intergenerational workforce might embody beyond the existing tensions.[4]

A Call to What Really Matters

What's important to understand in every example I've shared, and every story I've told, is that you have choice—even when it doesn't seem like it, even when it doesn't feel like it. When you can release the need to be everything to everyone all of the time, you begin to loosen the binds of not-enough-ness. You do not need to have everything; you can focus on what matters. And the great news about that is that you get to define what that is. You get to determine what's important in the who, what, when, where, why, and the how.

Overcoming scarcity is a deeply personal *and* universal opportunity. To shift the foundation of our ambition from desperation to inspiration requires greater trust and a commitment to be on the frontlines of our lives and work engaging with ourselves and each other differently. Our trust can be cultivated from many things, whether we root ourselves in ancient and indigenous wisdom that has offered alternative and more inclusive models for centuries, or in movements that have shown an unwavering commitment to social, economic, and environmental change.

Our commitment can also derive from challenging our ingrained reflexes to cling to what is no longer healthy even when it is profoundly familiar—to embrace uncomfortable change and cultivate the capacity to positively engage with the unknown in the name of what we desire.

When we consider our renegotiations from this place, we'll recognize that we live in a world of infinite possibilities. People, places, and opportunities will come and go. Some will triumph and some will falter—this is the nature of life which is ultimately designed to grow us—to make room for something better, to make *us* better as in more of who we really are.

Your Terms

1. As you consider your most important renegotiations, what are the things you absolutely want to hold on to? What are the things that you're willing to let go? Write about this.

2. Using my Seven-Step Process for releasing: Choose one area where you feel the most challenged and walk it through my Seven-Step Process. You can access it at www.movethecrowd .me/IA-resources.

For more downloadable tools and resources go to: www.move thecrowd.me/IA-resources.

Part VI

How to Renegotiate with the World

What becomes possible in the world happens through us. The more we consciously work toward our aspirations and visions from a more authentic, inspired, and accountable place, the greater opportunity we have to actually influence the larger shifts we'd like to see happen in our world.

One of the most compelling shifts we've experienced coming out of the Great Resignation is the call to greater meaning and purpose. So many of us looked out at the state of our world and determined that we would not spend another day doing work that did not in some way inspire us. Our incredible (and challenged) world is filled with opportunity. There are so many things that want to be newly created, peacefully solved, and reimagined. And now more than ever there are an infinite number of vehicles to support these efforts. Whether you feel called to solve a pressing challenge or fulfill an exciting new aspiration, whether you're taking the entrepreneurial path or engaging within a large established institution, invitations to improve the quality of our lives, our ventures, our work, and our world are all available to you.

In this final section, we'll consider what it actually means to be *influential* as in the architects and heroes of our own success story. From innovating new models to transforming existing systems with courage and care, we'll examine how to arrive at a new table ready to drive greater opportunity and impact in the lives of the organizations, teams, and individuals we serve.

Chapter 16

Renegotiating with the World: The "Yeah, But" Chapter

"The challenge lies in what we've been taught to define and measure as progress—we are looking at the wrong indicators."
—AH, Corporate Change Agent

You've worked on your game plan for reentry, you've begun having those crucial conversations, and maybe even some tough renegotiations. You've felt moments of inspiration but also really strong pushback. Then here come those lingering voices that are still challenging you. Despite that you've read Chapters 10 and 11 and its lessons about changing your mindset around change and giving yourself permission, you're still saying, "Yeah, yeah, this is all well and good, but get real!" You're saying, "Sure, some people can just ditch everything and start again, but I'm 48 years old!" You're saying, "I'd love to work more humane hours and stress less, but I have a family to support!" And what you're really asking is *how*—"How do I renegotiate when I still believe at some level that ... I just can't?"

This is our moment to address those remaining objections that have been so good at robbing you of the opportunity to make your greatest contribution.

You know, the stubborn ones that perpetually get in the way of you doing the work that you love and working in a way that inspires and excites you? Every reason you offer about why it's not possible becomes yet another nail in the coffin to your dreams and aspirations. You don't want this! I don't want this! So why don't we stare these babies down once and for all?

Yeah, okay ... but how?

One of the permissions we talked about in Chapter 11 was the permission to pursue. This chapter is all about the how-to, and I'll be sharing what people have actually done to renegotiate their work and their lives: road-tested moves, strategies, and solutions along with some food for your journey.

I know from experience: *everyone* can renegotiate. And everyone includes you. For inspiration, let's go back to John Jaso, the Major League Baseball player who (1) by all appearances, had it made, with a job and a life only a fool would walk away from, (2) was contractually obligated to do that job, never mind that he kept being "fired" (traded) *and* getting injured on the job *and* to be honest just didn't love what he was doing, and (3) walked away from pro baseball because he wanted to spend his life sailing; but more than sailing, he wanted a life that fulfilled him.

Again, I hear you: "Of course a professional athlete can change his life! He's a professional athlete! And a millionaire! I am neither of those things!" But to me the important part of Jaso's story isn't the goal. We all have different best-life scenarios: For some it might be sitting on a beach; for others, it might be having fun on the job and working with friendly and supportive colleagues. So what's instructive—and completely great—about Jaso's story isn't where he was going, but *how he got there*. And how he got there was by taking baby steps.

When his team was in a city with water and marinas, Jaso would go scouting for boats. In his spare time, he methodically figured out everything he needed to know about sailing. (Remember, this wannabe sailor had never actually sailed!) And he set about patiently and resourcefully learning what he needed to learn—by watching YouTube videos.

Baby steps! YouTube! Change is possible, y'all. I've seen thousands of times how the consistent, resourceful, and committed pursuit of a goal can take people from deep unhappiness to a place of great fulfillment—including *many* people you wouldn't think were in a position to call their own shots. The goal of this book is to help you join the ranks of these people. The goal of this chapter is to give you not just inspiration, but an array of inspiring examples that you are more than welcome to copy.

> Take Batina, who after 15 years in the fast paced world of hospitality and entertainment became passionate about the environment. After being invited on an international trip sponsored by a sustainability organization, she emerged with an exciting idea to develop a consultancy that would integrate the principles of clean living with ecotourism and luxury. One aspect of her business would focus on high end travelers offering unique curated experiences and the other would work with resorts to develop ecocentric programs to attract a more conscious consumer. She developed a slide deck and began hosting conversations with colleagues and former employers. Drawing on her marketing chops and her understanding of these intersecting worlds, she designed innovative trips and gatherings to foster a community built around these ideals - and found a way to make her services profitable.

Or Ronisha who brought her sales genius *in house* with a phenomenal tech company. Coming to the table with a desire for greater autonomy, creativity and the resources of a phenomenal team, Ronisha devised her ideal role. She wanted to share her brilliance, learn a ton about the next technological wave and cultivate the next level of her leadership. Next she reached out to 25 people in her trusted circle of colleagues and friends and asked if they knew of anyone who needed sales support. She didn't just give a synopsis of her resume; she laid out her full criteria for the kind of company she wanted to work for. Soon after she received a call from a friend at said tech company who needed help. What made her a yes? After doing her due diligence, she discovered that the firm not only shared her values but also held a deep commitment to creating a culture that made it one of the best places in the world to work. She signed on and hasn't looked back since.

Or Ilyana who after 25 years of fighting the good fight decided to retire early. She met with a financial advisor who helped her devise a budget that would make her savings last. She signed up for a YouTube course to teach her how to launch her own channel. And she's begun cultivating a new venture that would enable her to continue to share her expertise within her industry while also providing inspiring experiences and practical wisdom to awesome women of color over 55 years. She's still refining her revenue model, but having so much fun—traveling, learning, and connecting with potential collaborators and finding true joy and freedom in the work she loves.

Just like Gen Z, there's a whole new movement among Boomers called the third act, which is all about reclaiming their authenticity, leveraging their wisdom, and leaving a lasting legacy. And Ilyana was more than happy to join those ranks.

They Are YOU!

Every day, people like Ilyana are defying the doubts and renegotiating their lives in ways that create more joy, authenticity, and freedom. And every day, hardworking people just like you are discovering that they can too.

Walk of life, age, orientation, economics, physical ability—none of it is standing in the way of a whole new legion of people who are stepping forward in honor of what they truly want. They may not have all of the steps mapped out, and they may not have all of the answers about how it's going to look when it's all said and done, but they are walking forward nonetheless, intentionally moving toward that vision.

Now I want you to close your eyes and imagine that *they* are you. Think of even one time when you did what was right for you, when you stood up for yourself, when you renegotiated for your worth and it was good. What if that wasn't just one time 10 years ago? What if it was 90 percent of your experience instead of 10?

Now I want you to actually envision yourself sitting in the seat you want to occupy in your reimagined vision for your life and your work. I want you to see it, feel it, taste it. Now I want you to return to that place of stillness, the one we cultivated through the work of Reclaiming your narrative, through the work of Realigning with your truth, through the work of Reimagining your desired contribution, and through the work of your CPR—and I want you to ask (with your journal open):

What is one step I can take today to move me closer to this vision?

And I want you to listen ... then I want you to write down exactly what you hear.

Sometimes when we get guidance, one of two things can happen. It's so huge that we get overwhelmed because we have no idea how to get from where we are to wherever that is that we're imagining in our minds' eye—so we do nothing.

Our new response is going to be to *chunk it down*—make it smaller. To break the guidance out into tiny pieces so that it's doable and feasible for us. Don't know where to start? Then pose this next question...

What is the smallest version of this step I can take today that moves me toward my vision?

When Ciara, another beloved client of mine, wanted to make a change from her corporate world of engineering, it took her some time to figure out what was next.

Cooking had always been something she loved; she grew up in a home where food was important. "It was the way we loved one another," she said. As she began to explore her passion for supporting others—the journey kept leading her back to the kitchen—she started by devoting her time to learning all about various types of cuisine by studying recipes and practicing various kinds of cooking techniques on the weekends. She fed friends, her husband, even her baby cocker spaniel Ralph got to taste a few recipes! She used the feedback to tweak her style, build her confidence, and develop a wide array of cooking skills that could be applied to French, Italian, Asian, and American Continental cuisines. Her next step was to get clear about who she wanted to serve. This was also a journey of trial and error! She finally realized that she loved the idea of supporting busy families—honing in on executives with small children who had zero time but wanted to have a consistent healthy diet and regimen. Once she got clear on who she'd most enjoy serving, she researched platforms where she could promote her services, using everything from bulletin boards, to chef collectives, to Yelp and everything in between. She didn't need a ton of clients; she loved the idea of working for a few families at a time and having the ability to structure her time in such a way that she maintained her weekends off as well as having a "fun in the kitchen" day to just try new recipes. "What I noticed was how much I loved working for people who truly appreciated my efforts. At some point, this became a requirement for me." After she secured the right partnerships, she was able to negotiate sick time, vacation time, and wellness time with her families, which gave her the ability to take time off when the families traveled or when she and her family wanted to take a long weekend. Taking it one step at a time and one day at a time, she was able to create a life where she does what she loves and with people that she enjoys and admires and who are truly grateful for what she provides.

Other times, we get the guidance, but it doesn't make sense in our logical minds so we dismiss it—because we think it's inconsequential.

We've talked *a lot* about listening—particularly to yourself and how important it is. I often get the question, *Yeah, I hear myself talking, but how do I know it's "the me" I should be listening to?*

This brings me to Feliz, a brilliant yoga and meditation teacher who felt compelled to work with corporations to help them develop wellness initiatives for their employees. Feliz, a former senior vice president, knew how stressful the work could be for leaders at every level and wanted to create sanctuaries within organizational structures where people could truly decompress, rest, and restore. "When I first got the idea, I immediately dismissed it," she said. "I mean a residency in a corporation—focused on wellness? Who does this? No matter how much I tried to ignore the idea, it just wouldn't go away. One night I just sat down, took out my journal, and began to map out the whole thing." She designed a unique residency where she'd spend significant time within a company working to help create a culture of reset. Setting up beautiful movement and meditation rooms became an integral part of what she offered. "Once I created the vision for what I'd do, I just started talking about it—to friends, associates, people I met at networking events, at my nephew's bar mitzvah; you name it. I even offered complimentary experiences as an example of what I could offer until I landed my first residency." Once she got the gig, she launched her residency. She'd run a schedule of alternating yoga, sound healing, and meditation classes, as well as just opening up the space for quietude, rest, and relaxation. She held private sessions with executives in the early morning or late evening as requested to help them either tune up or wind down from a long stressful day.

"There was this moment, I remember, when I was leading a meditation for a specific executive team. They were working on a major project and everyone was stressed about the looming deadline. As I rang the mindfulness bell and looked around the room I was moved. *This is my life now*, I said to myself. Then I thought, imagine if I'd never followed the urge to even write this idea down? Who knows what I'd be doing."

If the guidance is moving you out of your comfort zone and into a place of greater joy, expression, and inspiration, then you know that it's a calling.

The Journey of 1,000 Miles

One of my favorite passages from the *Tao Te Ching* by Lao-tzu (the Stephen Mitchell translation) is verse 63 where it says to "think of the small as large and the few as many" and to "accomplish the great task by a series of small acts."

Every step that we take in the direction of what we aspire to achieve matters. When we endeavor to do great things, we will always be met by our cynicism. Its lack of familiarity with the genuine entertaining of our true ambitions can trigger lots of fear and doubt. Our work is to keep walking, to keep moving forward, to keep asking those ever-important questions that are rooted in who we want to be and how we want to live and work.

There are levels, stages, and even phases to renegotiating. We may not see all of the steps effortlessly unfold before us. We may only be given the path—one stone at a time. As we grow our capacity to trust, and as we build the muscles of greater courage and permission, we find our way and most importantly, the way finds us.

When I ask people today about their ambition and how it may be different today than it was five years ago, people are not as interested in back-burner-ing their dreams anymore. Especially when they feel the call to make a difference in the lives of others. The passion for new models and new ways of operating combined with the endless potential of avenues for realization provides just the right amount of fuel to encourage those initial steps in a new direction.

Another thing I'm observing as a primary motivator for how people are renegotiating is the call to greater personal respect and dignity. In the transformation of our ambitions the shift in the way we feel about ourselves is now moving front and center. You may be feeling this too!

"Yeah, but" can be so much easier to rely upon when you can't see all of the pieces or when money gets tight. I know, I've lived it; but the commitment to keep coming back to your new foundation *is* the practice. To take the steps you know how to take and to believe that the next part of the journey will show up right on time to meet you.

Your Terms

1. For the next 30 days in your journal, pose the question, *"What is one step I can take today to move me closer to this vision?"* Write down whatever you hear.
2. Then take that action.

For more downloadable tools and resources go to: www.move thecrowd.me/IA-resources.

Chapter 17

Who Wins? A Pep Talk to Send You on Your Way

"Enjoy this life because at some point, we will all be dust."

—Lily Carter

After all we've been through over the last five years (25 really)—the violence, the corruption, the polarization we witness day in and day out—we know that our system of work is begging to be reimagined. Formerly set up to produce winners and losers, we've seen very few of the one and many of the other. When we layer on an analysis of the state of our world, especially post-pandemic, it can be easy to assume that our renegotiations won't matter in the larger scheme of things. Even as we consider the implications of technology and the implied threat of the various forms of intelligence, it can be easy to believe that at some point *we* won't even matter.

And this is the part of the journey where I get to offer up one final challenge. Because when you're willing to renegotiate—reclaim, realign, and reimagine—even in the face of the most pressing challenges, something more profound and impactful becomes possible.

On an individual level, renegotiating leads to you becoming happier and in every way healthier. This in turn leads to improved relationships with your (chosen) family and friends and colleagues. And the communities, organizations, and workplaces you're a part of benefit greatly when you're able to contribute the best, most-invested, creative, and committed you instead of the beaten-down, demoralized, going-through-the-motions you.

Meet the New You

Now, what if I told you that this new you—this best you—just might change the world? It's true! Because when you renegotiate, you position yourself to *behave heroically*. On a daily basis. You can do things to foster a more humane and equitable work culture, which in turn starts to give us access to a more humane and equitable world. And when you show up as more humane and equitable, you inspire others to show up that way too!

When I speak of behaving heroically, I have zero interest in igniting your ego. What I mean is when you recognize the power of your own commitment and the potential, it positively influences and advances those around you. This commitment doesn't live in a title or a pay grade, and it doesn't demand that you become the biggest nor the loudest. It simply requires that you engage in the *practice* of actively honoring the renewed vision you hold for your life and your work—on a daily basis—and to see yourself as a living, breathing, active creator and contributor.

Think about it. When you renegotiate as in reclaim, realign, and reimagine your way to a better working life, you know firsthand the difference between the new you and the old you. New you is in the zone. Working at a very high level. Excited. Curious. Engaged. Showing up. Contributing.

For sure! But even new you can't do it all alone. You need colleagues and collaborators. And it only makes sense that you'd want them to be their best, most invested, creative, and committed selves too!

Now, I want to encourage you to also consider the larger ecosystems you operate inside of and the potential to hold a vision for *those* missions and *their* health. What would it be like if there was no enemy? No "them" and no "us?" What would be possible for the world and our system of work if we recognized that we are both stakeholders *and* shareholders in the efforts that drive growth and evolution, in other words, that we are all in this together?

This is why it's entirely likely that you're going to become a change-maker—an agent of change not just in your own life but for the benefit of others *and* our larger systems so that everybody truly can win. It doesn't matter where you choose to stand along the continuum of contribution. What matters is that you're willing to foster new and reimagined ways of operating, with more life-giving (regenerative) terms and conditions.

Of course, any conversation about who "wins" in work spaces needs to consider the impact that wounded and limiting ideologies, protocols, and structures have had on *all* of us. You may find that your renegotiation is central to this issue, and that makes it even more vital that others are inspired to stand with you.

Whether you choose to leverage technological innovation to bring about new ideas, greater efficiencies, or cutting-edge experiences or whether you choose to foster spaces that encourage greater physical, emotional, and financial health and well-being in the name of building greater access, resources, and capacity, this call to ensure that more people can thrive in their lives and work is essential—to *all* of our work.

201

Who Wins? A Pep Talk to Send You on Your Way

When I ask some of our greatest practitioners in the field of re-imagining work about the future, here's what they've had to say as we consider some of the most important frontiers for Renegotiation:

On Zero-Sum Thinking

"There is a fundamental rejection of the extractive model; it's simply not sustainable. There's a strong attachment to money which we don't have to let go of; we just need to expand what we are solving for. We can have money, we can build commercial success and value. WE CAN HAVE BOTH! We can build wealth for more people and build generative systems. It's the finite thinking we're shifting … where our level of consciousness is moving us more towards the infinite level of potential and possibilities. We are unlearning the fundamental belief that human and commercial thriving are not possible together."

—Christine Hildebrand, Business Strategist, Leadership Coach, and Founder/CEO, Cofinity Consulting

"How might our humanity shape capitalism and how might capitalism manifest our humanity? This has been the question that has most animated me. We have to reconcile this; there is no way that humanity is going to get there unless our economy and our humanity can find a way to mutually thrive."

—Raphael Bemporad,
Founding Partner and CEO, BBMG

"I believe another part of the evolution of our consciousness and the evolution of how we work together is the recognition of how much our differences are a part of our genius, not a threat."

—Lori Hanau, Founder and CEO,
Global Round Table Leadership

"If we all thought 500 years ahead what would we be doing differently? If we believed that everyone does better when everyone does better we'd make far more money if we took care of the planet in all of our decisions. This and we'd ensure the next 7 to 10 generations of people, planet, and profits. You can take the pie (as it is) or you can make the pie bigger and keep your same stake—you'll have a lot more if you do the latter. I don't want to go to Mars, I want to stay here."

—Michael C. Bush, CEO, Great Place To Work

On Artificial and Augmented Intelligence

"Contributors in companies and the marketplace have a profound opportunity before them—to explore the future of work through the lens of Augmented Intelligence. In what ways can AI make us more efficient and impactful in the way we work? Contributors who are willing to master these skills become very valuable in the marketplace—because they enable organizations and companies to become more profitable too!"

—Michael C. Bush, CEO, Great Place To Work

203

Who Wins? A Pep Talk to Send You on Your Way

"I think AI is great news for humans because it means we can focus on what we truly love—on what makes us uniquely human. By delegating mundane and tedious tasks to technology, we free up more space to be creative and innovative, and I believe that will ultimately make us even more valuable."

—Cheria Young, Founder & CEO, Grow There

"We need to stay in the driver's seat of our own creations. We need to continue to develop our awareness, our ability for vast perspectives in order to fully understand the implications of our innovations. Our consciousness IS distinct from AI and our human superpower."

—Christine Hildebrand, Business Strategist, Leadership Coach, and Founder/CEO, Cofinity Consulting

On Intergenerational Bridge Building

"The existence of multigenerational workforces is not anything new. However, listening to one another through the lens of each bringing value *is* new. We have an opportunity with Gen Z to appreciate that they are not the same as us 20 or 30 years ago. They are their own beings with their own perspectives and ideas, who've grown up in a totally different era. How can we see their newness? And as for our older generations, we've got a world of experience and lots of hard-earned wisdom (i.e. accumulated knowledge and skills with empathy and compassion—as defined by Dr. Maya Angelou). How do we invite and encourage the value of those insights to be seen and appreciated as well? Because both of us need to be willing to make the world better."

—Michael C. Bush, CEO, Great Place To Work

"Something else wants to happen. What will it require to have people to listen? I am so impressed by the young people. I think the leadership of our times is coming from younger, better, models of human beings."

—Michele Shay, Actor, Director, Chair of Performance, University of Southern California

On Transforming Systems

"You have to select in. You must know that you are selecting in to change the systems. You have to set your horizon line, you have to plant deep and fast, and at the end of each row you have to have your go bag ready! The systems will fight like hell to stay the same. So, you have to be clear about what you're here to do. You have to also be humble; you may only be able to change one part of *one* system. But you've got to lay the groundwork so that the person behind you can change the next thing."

—Nataki Garrett, Author, Award Winning Director, Artistic Leadership Advisor

"When it came down to the practice of sustainability my colleague and mentor Joseph Ingram really changed it for me. He said, 'You have been thinking that your employees are in service to you but it's the opposite.' What he meant was, you're in service to their health, to their values, to their growth and development; you're in service to their flourishing. He redesigned the entire company structure such that the flourishing of the team became the currency of success."

—Raphael Bemporad, Founding Partner, BBMG

205

Who Wins? A Pep Talk to Send You on Your Way

"Curiosity is your superpower, we've never been where we need to go. So we have to get curious and courageous to walk into some unknown territory."

—Jay Coen Gilbert, cofounder B Lab
and the B Corp movement, Imperative 21,
and White Men for Racial Justice

On the Individual and the Collective

"What I think is hiding in plain sight at every moment is to see ourselves as part of the whole. When we see ourselves in separation and the way we're treated in separation; and how that keeps giving us our own reflection as separate ... that we lose our imagination for wholeness and being a part of the whole. However, if we are not nurturing or nourishing ourselves, not giving ourselves the time and space, not seeing ourselves as part of the circle ... then it is not for the collective if it is not also for 'the me' as well."

—Lori Hanau, Founder and CEO,
Global Round Table Leadership

"What is missing in the current equation is the ensemble in leadership. We understand it in sports or music but we've not translated this model in the organizational world. This is about the model for Shared Leadership."

—Christine Hildebrand, Business Strategist,
Leadership Coach, and Founder/CEO, Cofinity
Consulting (speaking to the work of
Lori Hanau and Shared Leadership)

> "There is a need for a resurgence of the circle, the coffee-house, the civic square … spaces and actions that support genuine human-to-human connection."
>
> —Jay Coen Gilbert, cofounder, B Lab and the B Corp movement, Imperative 21, and White Men for Racial Justice

As a culture, we underestimate the value to everyone else when we as individuals are genuinely happy and fulfilled. And as individuals, we underestimate the value to us when others are healthy and whole.

Renegotiating teaches us to value things and *people* more accurately. To understand *what* matters—and that *we all* matter. And it teaches us that our world will be whatever we decide it is. We can use this profound moment in history to help architect new and more humane systems, policies, and structures. We can leverage the lessons from the pandemic into creating more inspired and relevant workplaces.

Who Else Is at the Table?

Renegotiating with our world means that we recognize that we are all inextricably linked. That when it comes to the nature of our work and our world, we don't have the luxury of silos.

When we endeavor to do our work, there is another stakeholder at the table: our mission. This serves as a symbolic representation of our ultimate contribution to the greater good. As we reimagine our systems and structures, it is imperative that we revisit our collective missions, whether we cross the threshold of our own ventures or lend our talents and gifts to larger institutions.

The mission deserves a seat at the table. It should also reserve the right to reclaim, realign, and reimagine. When we consider how we engage we must always ask the question: *What is my mission in relation*

207

Who Wins? A Pep Talk to Send You on Your Way

to this larger mission? What are my values in relation to these larger values? Where and how can we find alignment? Where and how are we able to foster greater alignment among others in service to the whole?

Beyond the typical commitments to delivering world class x, y, z and being "the best at p, d, q," what is possible for the organizations and entities we create and serve to encourage the next evolution of commitment and care—not just for the good of some, but for the good of all? Not just for the here and now, but for our future generations?

Renegotiation *is* happening, with all of us. Whether you connect to the stories of GangGang, John Jaso, Simone Biles, or even Giannis Antetokounmpo, who challenged the media in a press conference around the definition of failure and success, or with the dozens of individuals I've highlighted from our work at Move The Crowd, these shifts in perspective are creating new opportunities and new models for living and working.

It's not just about whether we go to the office or work from home. It's not about whether we are entrepreneurs or organizational contributors. It's not about that next promotion or that larger corner office. It's about creating a world of work that can actually work for all. It is within our grasp. What's broken in the system *is* fixable. Heck, the system itself is *re-imaginable*. In fact, change is not only possible, it's inevitable.

We have the capacity to craft a new kind of success story, one in which every kind of person and system can thrive. That's why I want you to Renegotiate. All of us deserve to reap the rewards of being our most authentic selves in service to our highest respective and collective contributions for now and for the centuries to come.

So let's get to the work that's really worth doing.

Trust me: It will be great.

Chapter 2

1. https://time.com/4621185/worker-productivity-countries/.
2. https://www.cultureamp.com/blog/40-hour-work-week#:~:text=Pros%20and%20cons%20of%20the%2040%2Dhour%20work%20week,-The%20case%20for&text=One%20thing%20we%20can%20say,than%2D8%2Dhour%20day.

Chapter 3

1. https://www.naacpldf.org/press-release/nikole-hannah-jones-issues-statement-on-decision-to-decline-tenure-offer-at-university-of-north-carolina-chapel-hill-and-to-accept-knight-chair-appointment-at-howard-university/.
2. https://www.mckinsey.com/capabilities/people-and-organizational-performance/our-insights/delivering-through-diversity.
3. https://www.mckinsey.com/~/media/mckinsey/featured%20insights/diversity%20and%20inclusion/women%20in%20the%20workplace%202022/women-in-the-workplace-2022.pdf.
4. https://www.nytimes.com/interactive/2020/09/09/us/powerful-people-race-us.html.
5. https://en.wikipedia.org/wiki/Robert_K._Merton.
6. https://www.theblackchildagenda.org/tackling-the-schools-to-prison-pipeline/.

7. https://www.adl.org/resources/lesson-plan/what-school-prison-pipeline?
psafe_param=1&gad_source=1&gclid=CjwKCAjwhIS0BhBqEiwADAUhc
1eMQeB9MffBS4o7QDX22uuG_iZLmRnBkeG4DuZBssdmxPgJB9co7
xoCSKIQAvD_BwE&gclsrc=aw.ds.

8. https://www.learningforjustice.org/magazine/spring-2013/the-school-to-
prison-pipeline#:~:text=The%20school%2Dto%2Dprison%20
pipeline%20starts%20.

9. https://lawjournalforsocialjustice.com/2021/03/29/the-poverty-to-prison-
pipeline/.

10. https://lawjournalforsocialjustice.com/2021/03/29/
the-poverty-to-prison-pipeline/.

11. https://prisonwriters.com/educate-not-incarcerate/?gad_source=1&gcli
d=CjwKCAjwhIS0BhBqEiwADAUhczpYqZW0gq-kNhWPkSF
ZhdIwXXSE4HnyGq-ylONGJvsqcg9exNA4FxoCV3sQAvD_BwE.

Chapter 4

1. https://www.deloitte.com/global/en/issues/work/genz-millennial-
survey.html?id=gx:2pm:3dp:4genzandmillennialsurvey2024:5GC100010
2:6hc:20240617::forbes.

2. https://www.shrm.org/topics-tools/news/inclusion-equity-diversity/
front-line-workers-quitting.

3. https://www.shrm.org/membership/hr-professional.

Chapter 5

1. https://youtu.be/ZtI4eH1U2rY?si=yaKQPv6mCMcJ5NG8.

2. https://time.com/6077128/naomi-osaka-essay-tokyo-olympics/.

3. https://www.nytimes.com/2023/09/06/sports/tennis/us-open-naomi-osaka
.html#:~:text=Osaka%2C%20the%20four%2Dtime%20Grand,to%20
compete%20again%20in%202024.&text=Naomi%20Osaka%20didn't%20
bring,Tennis%20Center%20on%20Wednesday%20afternoon.

4. https://www.cnn.com/2023/08/04/sport/simone-biles-gymnastics-
return-intl-spt/index.html.

5. https://www.nytimes.com/2021/07/28/sports/olympics/simone-biles-out.html.
6. https://www.nytimes.com/2023/02/14/sports/baseball/john-jaso.html.

Chapter 6

1. https://www.powherredefined.com/report/.

Chapter 9

1. https://www.nytimes.com/2022/11/29/arts/design/ganggang-racism-indianapolis-artists-venable.html.
2. https://www.nytimes.com/2021/02/13/arts/design/indianapolis-museum-job-posting.html.
3. https://www.flowresearchcollective.com/.

Chapter 10

1. https://gailstraub.com/.
2. https://worldbusiness.org/fellows/david-gershon/.

Chapter 15

1. B Corp Story: https://ryanhoneyman.medium.com/how-did-the-b-corp-movement-start-4f43ffb51649#:~:text=To%20that%20end%2C%20in%20 2006,that%20there%20is%20a%20way.&text=If%20you%20would%20 like%20to,Honeyman%20on%20Twitter%20at%20@honeymanconsult.
2. B Corp Stats: https://en.wikipedia.org/wiki/B_Corporation_(certification) #:~:text=This%20B%20Corp%20mark%20can,162%20industries%20 in%2096%20countries.
3. https://www.deloitte.com/global/en/issues/work/genz-millennial-survey.html?id=gx:2pm:3dp:4genzandmillennialsurvey2024:5GC100010 2:6hc:20240617::forbes.

4. https://www.google.com/search?q=gen+z+values+and+morals&sca_
   esv=7a77a74d7d9ae2f4&sca_upv=1&authuser=0&sxsrf=ADLYWILljF-bci
   kuuquH02NUIBH107L4jw%3A1727612614826&source=hp&ei=xkb5ZsL
   DMK68kPIPjcmmkQI&iflsig=AL9hbdgAAAAAZvlU1icZZSYdNLOkRuEV
   8zI7_bjfVx0N&oq=genz+values+&gs_lp=Egdnd3Mtd2l6IgxnZW56IH
   ZhbHVlcyAqAggCMgcQABiABBgNMgcQABiABBgNMgcQABiABBg
   NMgcQABiABBgNMgcQABiABBgNMgcQABiABBgNMgcQABiABBgNM
   gcQABiABBgNMggQABgWGAoYHjIGEAAYFhgeSOQ9UABYiCBwAHg
   AkAEAmAFUoAHYBqoBAjEyuAEByAEA-AEBmAIMoAKCB8ICChAjGIA
   EGCcYigXCAgoQABiABBhDGIoFwgIQEAAYgAQYsQMYQxiDA
   RiKBcICBBAjGCfCAhMQLhiABBjHARgnGIoFGI4FGK8BwgILEA
   AYgAQYkQIYigXCAg0QABiABBixAxhDGIoFwgIOEAAYgAQYsQMYgw
   EYigXCAg0QABiABBixAxgUGIcCwgIOEAAYgAQYkQIYsQMYigXCAgw
   QABiABBhDGIoFGArCAggQABiABBixA8ICBxAAGIAEGArCAgoQABiA
   BBixAxgKwgIFEAAYgATCAgsQLhiABBjHARivAZgDAJIHAjEyoAeaVw&
   sclient=gws-wiz.

Acknowledgments

Words cannot do justice to the level of gratitude I have for all of the voices that lent themselves to this book. I'm grateful for the deep wisdom shared in support of my own unfolding concepts, ideas, and perspectives and in honor of their own. This book was born out of the ashes of a meltdown-turned-revelation and with every introspective thought and phrase I felt humbled to bear witness to the frontlines of others' Renegotiations in all of its many splendid stages. Beyond my own observations and musings, this book represents a collective testimony not just to the past and present but for sure to the future of life and work and the desire we all share for it to be brighter, better, and more enlivening for us all.

From the boardroom to the frontlines, from entrepreneurship to the public sector, from Gen Z to pre Baby Boomer, with my entire heart, I want to thank you for allowing me to hear you.

To my beloved Essentials, Lily, Elena, and the women of LIFT, Michelle (Chief Visionary), Avah, Amanda, Mellie, Mariela and Christina; to my next generation Thought Leaders, Michele, Dana, Trina, Manish, Brit, Vanessa, Jeanette, Anh Minh, LeRhonda, Tatiana, Nataki, and Funmilayo; to my Corporate and Educational stewards, Amy, Cheria, Doug, Marcella, and Daisy; to my Conscious Captains of Industry, Michael, Jay, and Geeta; to my Venture Caps, Lenore and Nathalie; and Mission Driven pioneers, Lori, Christine, Maryanne, (both)Taras,

Melea, and Raphael—THANK YOU! And to all those who shared courageously and anonymously, I am so grateful for you.

To the brilliant advocates and researchers whose tireless labor gave birth to all of the statistics, research, analysis, and graphics incorporated in this book and who are cited in the footnotes and data highlight sections. Thank you!

To my brother in transformation, William Ury, for your deep kinship, unwavering inspiration, and profound observations that went into the foreword for this book. Thank you so much!

To my beloved editors, Deborah Way for her brilliant co-framing and turn of phrase, and the awesome "keep-me-on-track" Kim Wimpsett for your eagle eye and warm heart.

To my incredible agents at Park Fine—Celeste Fine and Jaidree Braddix—thank you for always fighting the good fight and for continuing to stand for powerful ideas that challenge the status quo.

To my amazing publishing team at Wiley—Cheryl, Michelle, Amanda—for your passion and dedication to this work and your meticulous and unwavering midwifing of this vision.

Thank you all so much for lending your gifts and for believing.

To my Move The Crowd family and mission-driven soul mates—Monika, Lillian, Regina, Calgary, Jimmy, Lovelee, Lavelle, Anna, Karen, Jim, Henry, Sue, Cynthia, Harlowe, Rebekah, Jhanai, Kazi, Rolando, Hedy, and all those who've cared for this mission and come before. To the incredible leaders we get to serve on a daily basis—thank you for your trust and belief in us.

To the homies, Ghana (BFF), Natalie, Koya, Niyc (CH Sisterhood), Vito and Anna and all of the amazing women from my nFormation and Born To Shine movements. You make it all worth doing.

Finally, to my foundation, the Greenes, Fletchers, Davises, the Hyltons, Allens, and the Kupfer-O'leary clan—I love you! And last but never least to my partner for life Corey S. Kupfer, and my sweet furry girl Maisie. I could not be me and do this without you. Thank you—eternally for always having my back, front, and side.

About the Author

Rha Goddess is an author and the founder and CEO of Move The Crowd. She is the entrepreneurial soul coach behind hundreds of breakthrough changemakers, cultural visionaries, and social entrepreneurs. Her mission? To revolutionize the way we live, work, play, and handle our business. From multiple *New York Times* bestsellers to multimillion-dollar social enterprises, Rha's unique methodology has empowered a new generation of conscious entrepreneurs and leaders to stay true, get paid, and do good. Luminaries include, multiple NYT best-selling authors, Gabrielle Bernstein; to Founder of Girls Who Code and Mom's First, Reshma Saujani; to Global Peace Negotiator and Founder of the Harvard School of Negotiation, William Ury; to the President and Co-Owner of the Sierra Nevada Corporation and a Forbes Top 10 Self Made Women, Eren Ozmen; to *Time* magazine's 100 Most Influential for 2023, Imara Jones, just to name a few.

Rha has also leveraged her innovative approach to support leadership development and organizational transformation initiatives for: Google, Lululemon, Delta, The B Team, Power To Fly, Fidelity, KBL—Eisner, AICPA, Harris & Rothenberg International, Girls Who Code, The Ford Foundation, The Nathan Cummings Foundation, The Leeway Foundation, The Embrey Foundation, Omega Institute, The Center for Court Innovation, NY Cares, NY Foundation for the Arts, and many more.

From the onset of her more than 30-year career as a cultural innovator, social impact strategist, and creative change agent, Rha has drawn on the power of creativity, culture, and community to move hearts, minds, and policy. Rha's work has focused on issues of racial justice and equality, electoral politics, offender aid and restoration, mental health, and youth and women's empowerment and contributed to initiatives that have impacted millions of lives. As CEO of Move The Crowd, Rha is galvanizing a movement of 3 million entrepreneurs dedicated to re-imagining "work" as a vehicle for creative expression, financial freedom, and societal transformation.

As a sought-after speaker, Rha has led the conversation around a "whole self" approach to entrepreneurial leadership as the key to a more just, harmonious, and sustainable economy and world. Her work has been featured in *Time* magazine, CNN, Forbes, Fast Company, *Ms.* magazine, *Variety*, *Essence*, *The Source*, *Redbook*, and the *Chicago Tribune*, among others. In 2014, Rha was chosen as a Top 10 Game Changer by *Muses & Visionaries* magazine. In 2017 Rha was chosen as one of 50 Founders to watch by *Essence* magazine. Additional awards and honors include Meet The Composer, the NPN Creative Fund, a semi-finalist for Do Something's Brick Award and a two-time semi-finalist for Leadership for a Changing World (nominated by V-DAY Movement Leader, Eve Ensler).

In January 2020, Rha's debut title *The Calling* was published to rave reviews with *Publisher's Weekly* touting, *"This easily implemented work will help anyone develop concrete goals and the tactics to see them through."* BMW selected *The Calling* as a feature for its 2022 Supplier Diversity Conference gathering of more than two thousand attendees.

In 2021, Rha launched nFormation, a first-of-its-kind membership platform created by Women of Color for Women of Color with longtime client and collaborator Deepa Purushothaman. As a vetted, membership-based community, nFormation sought to reimagine traditional power structures to not just help more women of color (WOC) take their seat at the table, but to change the way the table is formed. In that same year, nFormation launched its groundbreaking white paper on WOC and the future of work called PowHer redefined. The research, done in collaboration with the Billie Jean King Leadership Initiative, raised the voices of over 1,800 women and sought to provide a clear roadmap for how WOC might contribute to reimagining workplaces for the future and led to a TED talk with over 1.7 million views. Building on the legacy of this work, in 2023 Rha launched Born To Shine, an immersive mastermind community and initiative dedicated to advancing the leadership, innovation, and ideas of WOC at a time when the world needs it most. Its inaugural program, *The Emancipation Plan*, enables leaders to build authentic brands while making their greatest contributions in a way that is profitable and deeply impactful.

Index

40-hour workweek, legalization, 23

Accountability
  absence, 73–74
  courage, 172
Achievement, reimagining, 150
Actions, adoption, 5
Advocacy, usage, 107
Affirmations, 153–154
Agency
  erosion, 17
  sense, re-establishment, 83
Agreements, defining, 160
Alienation, feeling, 11, 17
Alignment. *See* Realignment
  challenges, 94
  examples, 126–127
Ambition
  cultivation, 143
  desperation, 177
  dysfunctional relationship, 4
  fear/doubt trigger, 197
  problem, 4–9

redemptive qualities, usage, 151
Angelou, Maya, Dr. 204
Anxiety
  confrontation, 101
  manifestation, 8
Arrangements, defining, 160
Artificial intelligence, usage, 203–204
Aspiration
  alignment, 144
  approach, 23
  confrontation, 101
  reimagining, 150
  usage, 121
Augmented intelligence, usage, 203–204
Authentic connection, invitation, 157
Authenticity
  absence, 73–74
  generation, 183–185
Autonomy
  Gen Z desire, 184–185

Autonomy (*Continued*)
 importance, 106
 increase, 192

"Back against the wall" types,
 127
Backstabbing, 43
B Corp (TBL ethos), 183
"Being in the zone," 109
Belief, function, 134
"Belly full" people, 127
Belonging, work (impact), 25
Bemporad, Raphael, 202, 205
Best-case scenarios, response,
 17–18
Best-life scenarios, differences,
 190
Biles, Simone (courage), 63
Bottom lines, 181–183
Boundaries, 158–161
 monitoring/maintenance,
 159
Brands, impact, 182–1823
Breaking point, reaching,
 101–102
Buckets, determination, 162
Burden of proof, shift, 31
Burnout, 48, 53
 conversations, 92
 understatement, 149
Bush, Michael, C. 204

Calendar, realignment, 164
Career
 reboot, 148–149
 wall, 12–13, 53
Caster Semenya, Mokgadi, 30
"Catching the spirit," 109
Change
 agent, 201
 idea, 122
 making, 194
 perception, 144
 possibility, 191
 discounting, 119–120
 process, 124–127
 readiness, 127–128
Character building experience,
 50
Childhood, retention, 16
Chunking, 194
Clance, Pauline, 69
Clients, stubbornness, 133–134
Coaching, potential, 139
Collaboration, usage, 179–181
Collaborators, connection, 192
Collective breaking points,
 witness, 51
Communications person, hiring,
 121–122
Community
 impact, 97–98
 mind, changing, 128–129

valuation, 184
work, relationship, 24–26
Company
  criteria, development, 149
  launch, 191
Compassion, knowledge/skills,
  204
Compensation
  negotiation, 173–174
  package, impact, 174
Completion (reclamation step),
  84–85
Conducive environment, 98–99,
  113
Confidence, increase, 174
Conscious decisions, making,
  164
Consciousness
  evolution, 203
  level, impact, 202
Constraints, release, 111
Context, Purpose, and Results
  (CPR), 167–168
  preparation, 174–175
Context, setting, 168–169
Contribution, making, 144
Conversations, cultivation, 175
Cooking, love, 194–195
Cooperation, usage, 179–181
Courage
  impact, 121
  witnessing, 140

Co-working spaces, return, 99
Creative economy, activation,
  107
Creativity, concepts, 108
Credibility
  dilemma, facing, 74
  drawing, 22
Crews, Terry (testimony), 61
Cynicism/realism, 120

Daily life
  quality, 99–100
  vision, bridging, 163
"Delivering On Diversity"
  (McKinsey report), 33
Demands, barrage, 8–9
Democracy, subversion, 46
Desires
  perception, 65–66
  voicing, 173–174
Dignity, work (impact), 25
Dillard, Annie, 161
Disappointments, carrying,
  20
Discipline, function, 101
Discrimination, 62
Disenfranchisement, 67, 72–74
Distraction, opportunity
  (differences), 162–163
Doubt
  casting, 31
  triggers, 197

Dream
    ability, 105–106
    achievement, 66
    approach, 23
    back-burner-ing, 198
    nightmare, relationship, 58
    strength, gathering, 108–110
Dream Team, obtaining, 174
Drive, reverence, 68

Economic insecurity, 44
Ecosystems, consideration, 201
"Educate Not Incarcerate"
    (Prison Writers article),
    37–38
Efforts, value (acknowledg-
    ment), 7
Ego, igniting (avoidance), 200
Elkington, John, 182
Empathy, knowledge/skills, 204
Employee-based initiative,
    occurrence, 44, 53
Employee dissatisfaction, 6
Enduring, habit, 123
Energization, reason, 171–172
Energy, truth (relationship),
    64–65
Enlightened Humility, 151
Entrepreneurship, problems,
    57–60
Environment, hostility (creation),
    30

Excitement
    feeling, 169
    sense, 157
Exclusion, 43
Executives, private sessions,
    196–197
Exhaustion, 48, 51
Existence, goals (impact), 4
Expectations, defining, 160
Experience
    foundation, 168–169
    quality, importance, 24
Expertise, sharing (continua-
    tion), 192
External realignment, 161–162
Extractive model, rejection, 202

"Faces of Power: 80% Are
    White" (graphic), 34
Failure
    perception, 50
    permission, 137
Fallout, experience, 49
Family
    dynamics, messiness, 21, 70
    emotional fabric, holding,
    49
Fatigue, conversations, 92
Favoritism, 43
Fears/regrets
    confrontation, 101, 140
    trigger, 197

Feedback
  need, 75
  usage, 195
Feelings
  pain/disappointment, 181
  return, 161
Feinstein, Dianne, 61
Financial security, work
      (impact), 25
Financial success, vision, 96
Financial viability, 95–96
Five redemptions, 156–157
Flow state, 108–109
Floyd, George, 17, 46, 50, 101
  DEI surge, 33
Focus, shift, 149–150
Food, sharing, 180
Forgiveness, 88
Freedom
  Gen Z desire, 184–185
  sense, 106
Free market, rupture, 25
Frontiers/horizons, exploration,
      109
Fulfillment, 96–97

Game plan
  development, 165
  setup, 155
GangGang, story, 106–108, 111,
      115, 208
Garrett, Nataki, 205

Gaslighting, 43
Generation Z (Gen Z)
  isolation/anxiety, 53–54
  radical sharing mentality, 184
  truth, 183–184
Generosity, values, 181–182
Gershon, David, 128
Gilbert, Jay Coen, 183, 206, 207
Giving up, 46
  quitting, contrast, 43, 54–55
Globalized agreement, 20–21
Goals
  achievement, 58, 66
  challenge, 20
Gossip/gatekeeping, 73
Great Gloom, 6
Great Recession, 6
Great Resignation, 5–6, 166
  disruption, 178
  exit, 187
  response, 8–9
Grieving process, 84
Growing Edge distinction, 128
Growth, vision, 59
Guardrails
  crash, 159
  setup, 155
Guidance, 195–196

Habits, adoption, 5
Hanau, Lori, 203, 206
Hannah-Jones, Nikole, 28, 29

Happiness, importance, 106
Hard work
    ethic, 21
    ethos, impact, 23
    goal, 20–22
    narrative, importance, 21–22
Health, 95
    challenge, 47
    impact, 7–8
Heroic behavior, 200
Hiding out, 67, 75–76
Hildebrand, Christine, 202, 204
Houlahan, Bart, 183
Human connection
    culture, deprioritization, 25
    fostering, 53–54
Humanity
    detachment, 18
    manifestation, capitalism
        (impact), 202
Human needs, access, 37
Hunger Project, 167

Identity, 45
    change, 35
    erosion, 17
    intersectionality, 37
    sense, re-establishment, 83
Identity-based violence, rise, 6
Imagination, loss, 206
Imagining, ability, 105–106,
        193

Imposter Phenomenon (Clance),
        69
Imposter syndrome, 67, 69–70
Incarcerated people, median
        income, 37
Incarceration rates, reduction, 38
Inclusivity, values, 181–182
Indignities, toleration, 22
Individualism, ethos, 50
Individuality, erosion, 17
Influence, power, 32
Information, access, 175
Innovation, 41
Inspiration, 189
Intentional ambition, 143–144
Intentional decisions, making,
        164
Intergenerational bridge
        building, 204–205
Internal barrier, 140–141
Internal obstacles, dismantling,
        132–133
Internal Renegotiation process
    design, 153
    intentionality, 155–156
Internal revelations/reckoning,
        51
Intimate relationships,
        consideration, 98
Inventory, realignment, 155–156
Investment, possibility
        (consideration), 139

Isolation
    challenges, 49
    feeling, 11
"It's O.K. to Not Be O.K"
        (Osaka), 62

Jaso, John (resignation), 63

Kassoy, Andrew, 183
Kilio Cha Haki, 179
Kondo, Marie, 82

Layoffs, initiation, 48
Leadership
    company change, 18
    ensemble, 206
    positions, 178
    role, alignment, 171
Liberation (reclamation step), 85
Life
    cessation, courage, 100–103
    curveballs, 150
    daily life, quality, 99–100
    headache, 59
    importance, 112–113
    living, process, 161–164
    problems, defining, 159–160
    quality, improvement, 92–93
    reclamation, 83–86
    reimagining, 161–162
    stage, change, 157–158
    walk of life, 193

Lifestyle, embracing, 68
Limitations, reinforcement, 134
LinkedIn, usage, 191
Listening, 175
    courage, 102
    depth, 172
    importance, 196–197
Logistics, management, 133–134
Love, concept, 108
Loving (reclamation step), 85–86
Low-grade exhaustion, 7–8

Makeshift studio, setup, 179
Mass shootings, rise, 6
Mental breakdown, Resignation
        (impact), 59
Mental/spiritual/emotional
        burnout/breakdown, 23
Merit, myth, 29–32
Meritocracy, argument, 29
Merton, Robert K., 36
#MeToo movement, 60, 62
Microaggressions, 43
Millennials, change (making),
        120
Mind, changing, 128–129
Mindset, change, 119
Misery, origins, 58
Mission
    importance, 207–208
    relationships, 207–208
    statement, 107

Mission-driven corporate
    leaders, immersive
    experiences, 191
Mission/reality, disconnects,
    148–149
Mitchell, Stephen, 197
Mobility, limitation, 51
Modern world, false perception
    (debunking), 181
Morale, problem, 148–149
Mothering, industry, 139–140
Movement, feeling, 126

Narrative
    control, 31
    discovery, 125
    dominance, 82
    examples, 125
    trauma, 87
Natural born leader, role,
    148–149
Nauta, Ninka, 179
Navigation, 79
    impact, 9–10, 12
    phase, 16
Negotiation, 79
    approaching, framework, 167
    attempt, 166
    confidence, increase, 174
    cost, 38–39
    feeling, 16

immersion, 57
old-school negotiation, 166
phase, 9–10, 12, 59, 80
process, 166
    design, potential, 166–167
standards, 19
Negotiation-resignation-
    renegotiation continuum,
    9
Networking events, 196
Non-enough-ness, binding (loos-
    ening), 185
Nonhierarchical leadership, 184

Objections, addressing, 189
Obstacle, meeting, 132
Opportunities, approach, 12
Organizations, impact, 182–183
Osaka, Naomi, 62
Ostracization, 73
Outages, confrontation, 94
Out of true (misalignment), 91
Ownership
    absence, 67, 72–74
    reclamation, 82–83

Pandemic
    quitting, 46–49
    women, challenges, 54
Passion, sense, 157
Past hurts, carrying, 20

People
    decompression/rest/restoration, 196
    types, 127
Perfection, obsession, 69
Permission, 189
    road, 138–140
    slip, signing, 131
    types, 135–138
Permission succeed/fail on your terms, 137
Permission to be clear, 135
Permission to be on the journey, 136–137
Permission to be supported, 138
Permission to pursue, 135–136, 190
Personal ethics, alignment (absence), 184
Personal/professional growth, challenges, 20
Pipeline problem, 33
Playing field, shift, 8–9
Playing safe/small, 67, 74–75
Poverty to Prison pipeline theory, 36–37
Power, origin, 34
Preparation, 174–175
Pride, work (impact), 25
Priorities, change, 10
Productivity, increase, 98
Programming, usage, 107

Promotion, 111
Public scrutiny, impact, 62
Purpose, 96–97. *See also* Context, Purpose, and Results
    alignment, 170–172
    sense, 110–111
    statement, 171
    vision, 97
    work
        impact, 25
        relationship, 24–26
Purpose-driven anxiety, discussion, 65

Quitting, 46–49
    giving up, distance, 43, 54–55
    identification, 52–54

Race to Be Myself, The (Caster), 30
Realignment, 91–92
    call, 93–94
    external realignment, 161–162
    initiation, 126
    involvement, 93
    process, 101, 103
    work, 193–194
Reality
    language reflection, 45
    stress, 7

"Real Reason Why Your Frontline Workers Are Quitting, The" (article), 54
Reclamation, 81, 89
  increase, 124
  mantras, 84–86
Redemptions, 145
Reentry, game plan/guardrails (setup), 155
Reimagining, 105, 208
  occurrence, 119–120
Relationships
  cultivation, 166
  impact, 97–98
  improvement, 199–200
  thriving, 98
Re-membering (reclamation step), 84
Renegotiation, 79–80, 153, 159
  education, 207
  frontiers, 94–100
  impact, 199–200
  importance, 11–13
  initiation, 123, 200–201
  internal Renegotiation process, design, 153
  opportunity, 99–100
  phase, 11–12
  process, 82, 148, 187
Renegotiator, identification, 160–161
Reset culture, 196

Resignation, 41, 44, 51, 57. See also Great Resignation
  breeding, 46
  contention, 123
  definition, 11
  epidemic, 23
  exploration, 96–97
  growth, 26
  phase, 10–11, 12, 65, 80
  sense, 66
Resignation 1.0, 45, 79
Resignation 2.0, 79
Resources, squandering, 162
Responsibility, absence, 73–74
Results. See Context, Purpose, and Results
  absence, responsibility (avoidance), 88
  achievement, 172–174
Retirement, decision, 192
Righteous competition, 67, 70–72
Rights, possession, 71
Risk aversion, 119–120
Rules, change, 31

Sacred Embodiment, 151
Sacred pause, experience, 158
Sacred work, 92–93
Sacrifice
  badge of honor, 22–24
  experiences, 19

requirement, 61–62
suffering, contrast, 22
Safety, work (relationship),
    24–26
Scapegoating, 73
Scarcity
    mindset, impact, 177–178
    overcoming, 185
    scare, overcoming, 177
Scarcity-based work culture,
    Great Resignation
    (impact), 178
Scenario, creation (chances), 161
School to Prison pipeline
    advocates, impact, 36
    theory, 36–37
Security, work (relationship),
    24–26
Self
    power, 148
    reintroduction, 156–158
Self-fulfilling prophecy, 36
Self-introductions, methods, 45
Self-medication, 51
Self-mistreatment, 18
Self-neglect, 51
Self-proof, desire/drive
    (recognition), 70
Self-reintroduction, 165
Self-renegotiation, 117
Services, promotion, 195
Sexual abuse/assault, cases, 62

Sexual harassment, existence,
    60–61
shaming, usage, 32
Sharing, depth, 172
Shay, Michele, 205
Shining Bright, 151
Sick time, negotiation, 195
Simplicity, values, 181–182
Six Frontiers exercise, 102
Space
    re-entering, 156
    sharing, experience, 180
Spiritual path, 108
Stability, temperamental need,
    44
Stakeholders, identification, 182
Standing Tall, 151
Status quo, preservation (fight),
    134
Stories
    created story, 117–118
    keeper, role, 89–90
    language, change, 83–84
    reclamation, 83–86
Straub, Gail, 128
Striving, cycle (continuation), 9
Struggle, knowledge
    (absence), 3
Subliminal messages, impact, 70
Success
    compensation package,
    impact, 174

Success (*Continued*)
  created story, 117–118
  definition
    examination, 161
    improvement, 105
  external trappings, 18–19
  failure, 27
  inherited definition, 34
  naming, 107–108
  permission, 137
  problems, 57
  sacrifice, 15
  standard, recognition,
    70
  story
    crafting, 208
    redefining, 110
  trauma, 60–62
  vision, 110
Superhumans, resignation
  (impact), 62–63
Support system, dysfunctional-
  ity, 162
Sustainability, 95–96
Systemic roadblocks, identification (difficulty), 38
Systems, transformation,
  205–206

Tao Te Ching (Lao-tzu),
  197
Team dynamics, problems,
  86–87

Technological innovation,
  leveraging, 201
Thriving, odds, 38–39
Thwarting, 27–28, 73
  personal feeling, 28–29
  popularity, 35–38
  secret operation, 32–33
  shaming, usage, 32
Time log, keeping, 162
Tolerance threshold, 44
Toleration, consideration, 87
Transparency generation,
  183–185
Trauma, conversations, 92
Trauma-triggered responses, 59
Triple bottom line (TBL) (3BL),
  182
  ethos, 183
True ambition, 143–144
  framework, 145f
Trust, cultivation, 185
Two-inch barriers, 131–132

Unapologetic Devotion, 151
Unhappiness, 57–58
Us-*versus*-them, 53

Vacation time, negotiation, 195
Validation, drawing, 22
Violations, 17
Virtual office, entry (dread), 122
Visceral experience, creation,
  111–112

Vision
    bridging, 163
Volunteering, time (absence),
    158
Vulnerability generation,
    183–185

Wanting, complications, 66–67
Well-being, 95
Wellness time, negotiation, 195
What, Who, Where, Why, When,
    How (five Ws and an H),
    111–115
Wholeness, imagination (loss),
    206
Wisdom, earning, 204
Work. *See* Hard work
    culture, occurrence, 44
    departure, 48
    emergence, 103
    enjoyment, 109–110
    evolution, 203
    foreshadowing, 3
    impact, 25
    joy/freedom, 192
    messages, receiving, 22
    process, 53
    quality, 52
    sacred work, 92–93
    safety/security/purpose/
        community, relationship,
        24–26

spaces, conversation, 201
stage, change, 157–158
system, ethos, 28–29
traditional system, 178
Workers, burnout, 5, 6
Workforce, entry, 33–34
Working process,
    transformation, 23–24
Workplace
    nonhierarchical leadership,
    184
    sexual harassment, existence,
    60–61
Workplace, toxicity, 43
Workweek (40-hour),
    legalization, 23
World, renegotiation, 187, 189,
    207
Wounded, journey, 148–151
Wounded/wounding ambition,
    65, 143–144
    journey, 86–90
    types, 67–76
Wounding, sense, 66
Wounds, 145
    redemptions, 146t–147t

Young, Cheria, 204

Zero-sum mentality, 53
Zero-sum thinking, 177,
    202–203